Contents

12

An _ g ιrrop is a policy manager at Age Concern England,
spє g in employment and age equality. He represents
AC ▪ 6 ℯ DTI's Age Advisory Group on the forthcoming age
dis tion legislation, and on the Equality and Diversity
Foɪ ich brings together national equality and human rights
orɡ 2 ons. He is co-author of *Age Discrimination* (Legal
Ac 6 up, 2006), a book aimed at advisers and lawyers. Prior
to - ᴦ ACE, Andrew was a researcher at the New Policy
Ins He lives in south London.

Su unro is an information specialist at Age Concern
En specialising in employment and education. She is
res ble for writing and updating the Age Concern factsheets
anɗ 1 rmation sheets in these areas, which can be obtained
by ng the website at www.ageconcern.org.uk. She has
prc training for advisers on the new age discrimination
laυ as written widely on the subject. Before joining Age
Co England, Susie worked as a solicitor in private practice
in ngham, specialising in employment law. She lives in
Bri n.

i

Acknowledgements

We would first like to thank all those involved in the production of this book, in particular Jenny Roberts and Becky Senior. Our thanks go to our colleagues Fran Gonsalves, Alban Hawksworth, Rudi Reeves, Nikki Squelch and Arthur Tanner; and also to Sandra Coulthard (Department for Work and Pensions), Laurie South (PRIME), Mike Stewart (Centre for Economic and Social Inclusion), Emily Holzhausen (Carers UK), Ro Lyon and Sue Ward for their comments on draft chapters of the book. Particular thanks to James Leo, partner at Coley & Tilley solicitors, for his helpful input. Finally, a big thank you to our partners Katie Ghose and Darren Woodhouse for all their help and support.

YOUR RIGHTS

working after 50

A guide to your employment options

Andrew Harrop and Susie Munro

First published in 2006 by Age Concern Books
1268 London Road, London, SW16 4ER, United Kingdom

www.ageconcern.org.uk/agediscrimination

ISBN-10: 0 86242 425 9
ISBN-13: 978 0 86242 425 1

A catalogue record for this book is available from the British Library.

Edited by Jenny Roberts
Jacket design by Red Stone

Introduction

At the last count there were more than seven million people over 50 years of age in work, and close to a million more looking for a job. If this includes you, *Your Rights: Working After 50* is here to tell you about your legal rights and help you make the most of your employment options.

In this book we have answered all the key questions you might need to ask yourself about working and seeking work. Questions like:

- What are your employment rights? Are you protected from age discrimination? How do you enforce your rights?

- Can you take action to boost your income today? What are your best options for increasing your pension income for when you retire?

- What happens if you are out of work and want a job? Where can you get help? How can you brush up your skills?

- What can you do to balance work with family life, caring responsibilities, or health concerns? What are the best options for leaving work on your terms?

- Is there more to work than being paid by other people? Could you set up in business on your own or become a volunteer?

Your Rights: Working After 50 is unique. We wrote it because we were frustrated that there was nowhere to get all the key facts about work in one straightforward guide, and so it brings together information that was previously available only from many different books and websites. While much of the information is relevant to adults of all ages, this book is written specifically for people over the age of 50 and this is reflected in our decisions about what to include and what to leave out. For instance we've omitted information on employment rights for young adults and parents – with apologies to older mums and dads. On the other hand there's lots of information about issues that tend to affect people in work after 50, such as making the transition to retirement, coping with health problems and combining work with caring for relatives.

With such a wide range of topics to cover we haven't tried to have the last word on everything. But throughout the book we outline the basics you'll need to know to get by, and point you to other sources of information if you want to find out more. Contact details for all the organisations appearing in bold, as well as for other relevant organisations, can be found in the 'List of useful organisations' section at the back of the book.

Why now? *Your Rights: Working After 50* is published to coincide with the new law protecting people against age discrimination in the workplace. In October 2006 the Employment Equality (Age) Regulations 2006, Britain's first ever age discrimination law, came into force, offering protection to adults of all ages from being treated unfairly because of their age. Traditionally age discrimination has been seen as rather less important than other forms of prejudice like racism, sexism or discrimination against disabled people. But times have moved on.

Age discrimination is reported more widely than any other form of discrimination – by more than a quarter of adults in a recent survey for Age Concern – and it has really serious consequences for many people working after 50. Around one in ten employers openly admit to using age in their criteria for selecting recruits, and it's likely that this figure is just the tip of the iceberg. Age discrimination can result in some people being unable to find work at all and, more commonly, to skilled and experienced employees being forced to accept jobs far beneath their abilities. It all adds up to a huge waste of talent, as well as being a form of injustice that we simply shouldn't accept.

The Employment Equality (Age) Regulations 2006 provide adults of all ages with protection from age discrimination in relation to work and learning. But from the perspective of people over 50 the new law is not perfect, as the government drafted the legislation with one eye to the needs of cautious employers. This means there are still some situations where you can be discriminated against.

With complicated new rights on age discrimination, we thought it was essential that there was a guide to help people understand the law. But this book is about much more than age discrimination. It is a comprehensive toolkit for people over 50, because we recognise that tackling discrimination is just one part of the jigsaw for making the most of working life.

Mature workers are no longer at the margins of the labour market. When the economy was faltering, 20 or 30 years ago, it was accepted that people should stop working early to make way for younger adults. Today that's all changed. Over one quarter of the workforce is over 50 and there are now more than a million people over state pension age in work, with more and more people saying they want to work for longer. Life expectancy is rising so there are also financial realities to deal with. Longer life expectancy means that pension incomes have to stretch further. The problems facing many occupational pension schemes and the falling incomes of personal pension annuities have been well documented in the media. In this changing world, working for longer is often a necessary investment to secure a decent retirement income.

Your Rights: Working After 50 is here to help you get the best from whatever situation you're facing, whether you are in or out of work. From job interviews to retirement, this book tells you what to expect, what your rights are, and how to put them into practice. We hope that you find it helpful.

Andrew Harrop and Susie Munro

Age Discrimination
and the Law

Most of us are familiar with the concept of discrimination
when it comes to race and sex: unfair treatment at work
on these grounds has been unlawful since the 1960s and 1970s.
But the idea of outlawing age discrimination is relatively new
in this country.

For some employers, the new law may take some getting used to.
Age discrimination is still entrenched in many business practices,
and employers will have to learn to avoid making decisions
on the basis of ageist prejudice. You might see some alarmist
media stories telling you that we will no longer be able to send
birthday cards at work that make fun of a colleague's age (in fact,
it's very unlikely this would be unlawful). But it's important to
recognise that, as you may have already experienced yourself,
age discrimination can have extremely damaging effects for
individuals, for society, and – as employers and the government
are realising – for the economy.

Whether it's a question of being overlooked for training or a
promotion, or not getting an interview despite having the perfect
qualifications for the job, or being forced to retire, the truth is
that age discrimination is a problem that affects many of us.

The good news is that now there's something you can do about it.

This chapter will explain the legislation that has been introduced to combat age discrimination in the workplace, what its limitations are, and what it means for you.

Historically there has been very little protection for older workers in the UK. You could be turned down for a job for being too old, or selected for redundancy ahead of younger colleagues, just because of your age, and the law wouldn't be able to help you. There was an upper age limit to the right to claim unfair dismissal – either age 65 or the employer's normal retirement age, which they could set at any age they chose. Once you reached this age they could dismiss you without having a fair reason.

However, on 1 October 2006, protection against age discrimination was introduced for the first time in Britain. The Employment Equality (Age) Regulations 2006 provide new rights for people of all ages, in the areas of employment, education and training.

The new law applies to people of any age and so younger people are also protected from discrimination. Unfortunately, however, due to a number of exemptions, the protection given to people over 65 by the new law is far more limited than the rights people enjoy up to 65. Also, the law does not apply to the provision of goods and services so it is still lawful to discriminate on the grounds of age in these areas. For example, insurance companies can continue to set higher premiums for older people.

Most of this chapter refers to the duties and rights of employers and employees. However, most of the same rights and duties also apply when talking about training and education. This will be discussed on pages 13–15.

WHAT IS DISCRIMINATION?

It is now unlawful for employers to discriminate against their employees on grounds of age, in any area of the employment relationship, unless the discrimination can be justified or it is covered by an exception under the new law (see "Justifying discrimination"). This applies to recruitment, terms and conditions, employment benefits, training, promotion, dismissal and redundancy. There are different types of discrimination, explained below, which cover the different ways in which someone can be treated unfairly or put at a disadvantage because of their age.

Discrimination can either be direct or indirect. *Direct discrimination* means treating you less favourably than others would be treated, because of your age. For example, if an organisation refuses places on a training course to employees aged over 55, this would be direct discrimination. Similarly, it would be direct discrimination if an organisation had a practice of only hiring staff aged under 40, even if this was not official company policy.

Direct discrimination is also unlawful if you are treated less favourably on the grounds of your apparent age. This means that if you appear to be older or younger than you actually are, you are still protected against discrimination. Your actual age is irrelevant.

Indirect discrimination means having a policy or practice which puts people of a certain age group at a disadvantage, compared with other people. To succeed with a claim for indirect discrimination you have to show that more people in your particular age group are disadvantaged than people in other age groups. For example, a requirement that candidates for a position have five years' managerial experience would be indirect discrimination against people under around 25, as they would be less likely than older people to have had a chance to gain this amount of experience at this level. An employer may be able to justify this discrimination, if it was genuinely necessary for the person doing the job to have the experience. See below for information about justifying discrimination. If candidates for a job were required to have GCSEs, then this could be another example of indirect discrimination, this time against older people, who are less likely to have these qualifications, which did not exist when they were at school. Instead, employers should accept equivalent qualifications, such as GCE 'O levels'.

So with direct discrimination, people of different ages are treated differently, putting one person or group at a disadvantage. On the other hand, with indirect discrimination, everyone is treated the same, but the effect is that one group is put at a disadvantage. Direct discrimination can be easier to recognise than indirect, where people may not realise that their actions are discriminatory. This is why the new law is so important; it challenges not only those actions that are clearly unfair to older people, but also those insidious habits of thinking and acting that frequently put them at a disadvantage in society.

JUSTIFYING DISCRIMINATION

Discrimination will be unlawful unless the employer can show that it is justified, or it is covered by an exception. These exceptions will be looked at on pages 9–13.

To be able to justify doing something which would otherwise be discriminatory, an employer has to show with evidence that what they are doing is a proportionate means of achieving a legitimate aim.

A 'legitimate aim' might be something like protecting the health and safety of employees or the public, or ensuring the employee is in the job for a reasonable time before they retire. To show that what they are doing is proportionate, the employer must demonstrate that it is appropriate and necessary in order to achieve that aim. To do this, they would have to show that what they are doing does actually achieve the aim; that there would be no alternative, less discriminatory, way of achieving the aim; and that the importance of the aim outweighs the harmful effect of the discrimination.

For example, an employer could argue that they were justified in only recruiting people under a certain age if there was a long training period before the employee could start doing the job. If the training would take two years and the employer used a normal retirement age of 65, they might wish to set an age limit of 61 for entry to the training, with the aim of having the employee in position for a reasonable length of time before retirement. The employer would have to justify the age limit, in terms of the length and cost of training the employee, balanced against the time it would take to recoup these costs. They would also have to take into account the fact that there is no guarantee that younger employees would stay with the employer for any length of time after training either. Whether such justifications are accepted will always depend on the individual circumstances of each case.

If your employer tells you that a practice is justified, you don't need to take their word for it; if you think you're being treated unfairly, seek advice. Only an employment tribunal can decide whether something is justified, and they look at each case on an individual basis.

One major difference between the law on age discrimination and previous laws outlawing discrimination on the grounds of race, sex, disability, sexual orientation, and religion or belief is that both indirect and direct discrimination are potentially justifiable when it comes to age. With the other anti-discrimination laws you cannot justify direct discrimination.

If you think about this in terms of race discrimination, under the Race Relations Act, it would never be possible for an employer to justify a policy of, for example, selecting people for redundancy on the basis of their race. When drafting the age legislation, however, the Government has accepted that there may be some circumstances where it will be necessary and appropriate to treat somebody less favourably because of their age.

HARASSMENT

Harassment on the grounds of age is also made unlawful under the new law. The legal meaning of harassment in this context is *unwanted conduct, on the grounds of age, which has the purpose or effect of violating another person's dignity, or of creating an intimidating, hostile, degrading, humiliating, or offensive environment for them.* For example, if an employee in her late 60s has colleagues who make jokes about her age that she finds offensive, or exclude her from social events because of her age, this could be harassment. Harassment does not have to be based on your own age; it could be based on the age of someone you are associated with. For example, if colleagues make offensive jokes about your partner because your partner is much older than you, this could be unlawful harassment.

For conduct to amount to harassment, it must be reasonable to consider that it would have the effect of being intimidating, offensive, etc, taking into account the perception of the person making the complaint, and all other circumstances. This means that when deciding whether something is harassment in the legal sense, an employment tribunal would consider whether it was reasonable for the particular person to be offended, or whether they are being unreasonably oversensitive to the behaviour.

This may be a difficult judgement to make when you think of all the jokes and comments that fly around the workplace, many of which are based on age. It's also complicated by the fact that the offending behaviour is sometimes caused by accident, with people not realising how offensive their jokes can be. However, not *intending* to cause offence doesn't constitute an excuse in the eyes of a tribunal. Even is someone doesn't mean to upset you, their behaviour can still amount to harassment.

It's nearly always worth trying to resolve an issue of harassment before making an official complaint. First, ask yourself if the person in question is aware of how their behaviour is affecting you. A calm conversation might be all it takes to change the way they behave for good. You should consider why you found the behaviour offensive and why you think it's more than someone of any age should be expected to tolerate at work. This means examining your own sensitivities and your motives for taking action. For more information on resolving disputes see chapter 4.

If you make an age discrimination claim following harassment by your colleagues, your employer could be found liable to pay compensation, unless they can show they took steps to prevent the harassment occurring.

VICTIMISATION

Victimisation in this context has a legal meaning which is different from the everyday use of the word. It does not mean being picked on or treated unfairly because of your age, although this could be counted as harassment or direct discrimination. Victimisation means being treated unfairly as a result of your making a complaint or allegation of age discrimination, or giving evidence to support someone else's complaint.

It could be that you have complained to your manager that you think you've been discriminated against because of your age, and your manager then treats you unfairly as a result of the complaint, for example by demoting you or giving you a poor appraisal. You would have a claim for victimisation as well as a potential claim for the original discrimination.

Or it could be that you have gone as far as starting an age discrimination claim at the tribunal, and you are then put at a disadvantage by your employer, for example by being turned down for a promotion you would otherwise have got, or being forced to work a less favourable shift pattern. The idea behind the law is to make it easier for people to speak out, by protecting them when they do. You are even protected if you have not yet made a complaint, but your employer believes you are about to do so.

It is frequently difficult to gather evidence of discrimination and you often need support from colleagues who may have witnessed the incidents in question. Understandably, colleagues are often reluctant to give evidence, as they fear they may themselves become a target for unfair treatment by the employer. The law offers protection to people in this situation, as, if they suffer a disadvantage at the hands of their employer, for example being harassed at work or even dismissed, they can themselves claim compensation for victimisation.

RETIREMENT AND THE LAW

The new regulations introduce a 'default retirement age' of 65. The rules in the regulations set out when a retirement will amount to age discrimination, or unfair dismissal, or both (see chapter 3 for more information).

Generally speaking, the 'default retirement age' means that if you have reached your 65th birthday – or your employer's normal retirement date if this is later – it will be lawful for your employer to force you to retire, as long as they give you between six and twelve months' notice, give you an opportunity to request to continue working, and follow the correct procedure if you do make such a request.

If you are under 65, it will usually be unlawful for your employer to force you to retire, unless they can justify a lower retirement age. Employers who require their employees to be physically fit – for example firefighters or oil rig workers – may attempt to justify a retirement age below 65, arguing that it is appropriate and necessary to retire workers before 65 to meet health and safety aims. However, they would have to show that there was no less discriminatory way of achieving this aim (such as introducing fitness testing), either for all workers, or for those over a certain age, rather than automatically dismissing people at that age. Again, the question of whether retirement ages below 65 are justified will be down to the employment tribunal to decide, on a case-by-case basis.

Chapter 3 goes into much more detail on the changes to retirement procedures, and the right to request to continue working.

EXCEPTIONS TO THE RULE

There are a number of exceptions included in the regulations which mean that age discrimination will be allowed in some circumstances. There is a difference between the exceptions to the law and the concept of justifying discrimination. The exceptions apply only in the circumstances set out in the regulations. If none of the exceptions apply, the employer will still have a chance to argue that the discrimination is justified and should be allowed.

Recruitment

For older people, perhaps the most important exception relates to the recruitment of people over 65. It will be lawful for most employers to refuse a job to anyone over 65, or over the employer's set retirement age (whichever is higher), without having to justify it, even if it is a decision based entirely on the person's age. The exemption extends to anyone within six months of their 65th birthday, or the employer's normal retirement age. So if an employer who has not set a normal retirement age receives a job application from someone who is over 65, or who will turn 65 within the next six months, they can decide not to consider that person for the job.

Similarly, an employer who has set a normal retirement age of 67 would lawfully be able to reject anyone over 67, or within six months of their 67th birthday. But an employer who has set a retirement age of lower than 65 would have to be able to justify not hiring someone under that retirement age; they would not be able to rely on the exception.

If you still have more than six months to your 65th birthday, or the normal retirement age for the job for which you are applying, it will be unlawful for the employer to reject you for the position because you are too old (or too young), unless this can be justified, or it falls under the Genuine Occupational Requirement exception. So, in principle, age should not be a relevant consideration in the recruitment decision for most jobs.

GENUINE OCCUPATIONAL REQUIREMENT

In some very limited circumstances, an employer can set age limits when looking to hire people for a particular job. This will only be lawful if age is a genuine requirement for the position. This part of the law mirrors similar exceptions in other discrimination law on race, sex and disability, etc. For example, in the context of sex discrimination law, it could be a genuine occupational requirement for staff at a women's refuge to be female. There will probably be very few circumstances where age will be a genuine requirement for a job. The requirement for someone to be of a certain age should not be confused with a requirement for someone to be physically fit. So, for example, an employer might set a maximum age limit of 60 for a job as a scaffolder, arguing that age was a genuine occupational requirement, as they needed the person to be physically fit. In this example the requirement would actually be for a fit person, not for a person of a particular age, and so the employer would probably not succeed with their argument that age was an occupational requirement, although they might be able to show that the age limit was justified.

The example usually given where having a characteristic related to a particular age will be a genuine occupational requirement is for acting jobs where authenticity requires that an actor playing a particular role looks a suitable age. Unlike the laws on sex and race discrimination, the age discrimination regulations do not set out the circumstances in which having a characteristic related to age could be a genuine occupational requirement. As with justification, it will be for the employment tribunal to decide questions such as this.

It will not automatically be unlawful age discrimination for an employer to ask for your date of birth during the recruitment process. However, if you believe that you have been rejected for a job on the grounds of your age, you could use the fact that the employer asked for your date of birth as evidence for an age discrimination claim. An employer who can show that the person making the decision neither asked for nor knew your age would be in a much stronger position to defend a claim.

It is good practice for employers to remove the date of birth from the application form and ask for this instead on a separate equal opportunities monitoring form, along with information about the applicant's race and any disabilities, etc. This form should not be seen by the people deciding who to shortlist for interview or who to hire. Again, this is not required by the law, it is just an example of what could be seen as best practice for employers. Of course, it will often be possible to calculate someone's approximate age by looking at their education and work history. Some employers are looking at moving to competency-based application forms, which avoid reference to dates and time periods entirely. However, employers will usually need to know your date of birth for administrative purposes and it will not be unlawful for them to ask for it.

Length of service benefits

An example of a length of service benefit is extra holiday entitlement after a certain number of years' service.

In theory, this kind of benefit indirectly discriminates against younger workers, as they are less likely to have been with an

11

employer long enough to qualify for the benefit. Few people would think to argue such a case and most workers wouldn't want to see these benefits discontinued. So an exception is included in the law to allow employers to continue with this type of policy in most circumstances. The law says that if the length of service required for entitlement to a benefit (including a pension benefit) is five years or less, it will automatically be lawful. For any requirement of more than five years, the employer has to show that it is expected to meet a business need, for example encouraging loyalty, motivating workers or rewarding experience. This is an easier test for employers to meet than the normal test for justifying discrimination, and it is therefore hoped that employers will continue to offer this type of benefit to their workers.

If your employer tries to withdraw a benefit linked to length of service, or uses the age discrimination regulations as an excuse for not introducing new ones, you can point out that there is an exception to the law designed to protect these benefits.

Positive action

Positive action here means doing something to prevent or compensate for disadvantages experienced by people of a particular age group. There are two areas where this will be allowed. The first is when giving people access to training and education. So, for example, an IT course for people over 60 may be lawful if the course provider can show that this age group faces a disadvantage in this area. Second, positive action will be lawful when encouraging people to take up employment opportunities. This means that advertising for a position can be specifically targeted at a particular age group, if they would otherwise be at a disadvantage, in order to encourage them to apply for the job. It would not be lawful to use positive action to refuse employment to people who are not in the targeted age group (this would be positive discrimination), as the exception only relates to encouraging people to take up employment opportunities, not deciding who ultimately gets the job. So positive action isn't the same thing as positive discrimination (which would be unlawful unless it could be justified).

Statutory authority

Certain laws exist which set age requirements for certain activities, for example getting a licence to serve alcohol. Employers will have to stick to those laws and will be able to rely on them as a defence against an accusation of age discrimination. So, for example, an employer would not be expected to hire someone for a driver's job if they weren't old enough to hold the relevant licence.

UPPER AGE LIMITS

Before the new law came into force, there were upper age limits to some employment rights. Effectively, the law stopped protecting you when you got past a certain age. One very positive change brought about by the new law is that the upper age limit for eligibility to claim unfair dismissal, which was previously age 65 or your employer's normal retirement age, has been removed, as has the upper age limit for claiming a statutory redundancy payment.

The upper age limit has also been removed for statutory sick pay. Before the introduction of the age discrimination regulations, you could not get statutory sick pay after the age of 65 but this is now no longer the case.

TRAINING AND EDUCATION

The age discrimination law also applies to some areas of education and training. All courses provided by universities or further education colleges will be covered, as will training provided by other organisations which aims to improve work-related skills, but school-age education will not be covered.

It's important to note that, as well as covering training provided by employers to their employees, the law also protects those who are currently out of work. In addition, it covers providers of career guidance and professional qualifications bodies. If you are in any doubt about whether you may have protection under the law, you should seek advice about your circumstances.

This means that education and training providers will not be able to set age limits for entry onto a course, unless they can justify doing so, or it is covered by an exception under the law, such as positive action (discussed earlier in this chapter).

As well as age limits for entry, any age limits for access to benefits or services related to education or training will be unlawful unless justified or exempt. For example, education establishments which provide residential accommodation for students will have to make this available to all ages, unless they can justify not doing so.

The government has stated that student grants, loans, bursaries and scholarships are not covered by the age regulations. Age limits for student loans and other government support will remain in place. This is an area where the government's interpretation of the law could be challenged through the courts.

If you think you have been discriminated against in relation to education, for example if you have been refused a place on a course and you believe this was because of your age, you may be able to take legal action against the course provider. This would be through the county court (or sheriff court in Scotland), rather than the employment tribunal. However, as with employment disputes, it is almost always worth trying to resolve the problem informally before starting a claim. You can use the questionnaire procedure under the regulations to request information from the course provider that you would otherwise not have access to. For example, you could ask for statistics on the ages of people on the course you were turned down for and this will help you assess the situation to see if it appears that discrimination is taking place. For details of the questionnaire procedure, see chapter 5.

Recent government policy has led to cuts in funding for adult education courses. Resources are concentrated on younger people, and on basic skills such as literacy and numeracy. You may have seen local adult education courses being dropped, or fees being increased because of this. There is therefore a conflict between the competing government policies of concentrating funding for education on younger people, and of ensuring that older people are not denied access to education and training opportunities.

PROVING AGE DISCRIMINATION

The law recognises that employees will rarely have conclusive proof that they have been discriminated against. Employers are unlikely to admit it, or have kept written records, and colleagues may be reluctant to speak out if they have witnessed something.

To succeed in claiming age discrimination you need enough evidence to show that you *could* have been discriminated against. If you can establish this, it is then for the employer to prove that they did not discriminate against you.

COMMISSION FOR EQUALITY AND HUMAN RIGHTS

In October 2007, a new body called the **Commission for Equality and Human Rights** (CEHR) will begin work. The role of the Commission will be to promote equality and tackle discrimination on all grounds currently covered by legislation – age, disability, gender, race, religion or belief, and sexual orientation. It will also be responsible for promoting and protecting human rights. The CEHR will replace the three existing equality commissions: the Equal Opportunities Commission, the **Disability Rights Commission**, and the Commission for Racial Equality. From October 2007, the CEHR will have responsibility for promoting and enforcing the law on age discrimination, including providing advice and information on the law. It is likely to offer information through a national helpline and on its website. However, it will not have the resources to provide individual legal advice or representation, except in a tiny handful of cases.

Your Rights at Work

This chapter looks at some of the specific rights you may have relating to your work. It is not possible to cover all employment rights here, for example parental rights such as maternity pay are beyond the scope of this book. The chapter aims to give you an overview of particular rights which may be relevant to you if you are over the age of 50. For information on how to enforce these rights see chapter 5.

STATUTORY AND CONTRACTUAL RIGHTS

Your employment rights come from two different sources. There are minimum statutory rights that you have under various pieces of employment legislation, sometimes originating in European law. Examples of statutory rights are the right to at least four weeks' annual leave, the right not to be unfairly dismissed and the right to be paid the national minimum wage.

The other source of employment rights is your contract. Even if you don't have a written contract with your employer, you still have contractual rights. These will be drawn from various sources, such as the wording of the original job advert for your position, which would probably have given some detail of the terms of the job; any letter sent to you confirming your appointment and detailing terms and conditions of employment; the staff handbook, if there is one; your job description; and importantly, any rights that have been established through custom and practice. This means that any policies or practices that your employer has consistently applied over a period of time can form part of your contract. For example, if in practice all employees are paid full sick pay for the first month's absence, this could be a contractual right, even if it is not written down anywhere.

The terms and conditions of your employment set out your rights and responsibilities at work; for example, how much you are paid and what hours you have to work. Details of some of the main terms and conditions are given later in this chapter.

Your employer must give you a written statement of the *terms and conditions* of your employment, within two months of you starting work. This isn't strictly the same as your employment contract, but is evidence of what is agreed under your contract. The statement should give details of the main terms, including when the employment began; how much you will be paid, and when payment will be made; your hours of work; your holiday entitlement; your job title; your normal place of work; pension scheme details; notice entitlement; and entitlement to sick pay. If your employer refuses to give you a written statement of the terms of your employment, you can apply to the employment tribunal, who will decide what terms have been agreed by looking at the employment relationship. This would usually only happen if you have got into a dispute with your employer, but you have the right to request the written statement of terms and conditions at any time.

Statutory rights often set out *minimum* requirements for employers to stick to. For example, there is a statutory minimum amount of notice that your employer must give you. If your employer tries to give you less than the minimum amount, they will be acting unlawfully, even if the lower amount is set out in your contract.

Many employers give their employees more generous rights in their contracts than the statutory minimum: for example, a longer notice period or a higher redundancy payment. In this case the employer must adhere to the contractual right, and if they try to give you only the statutory minimum they will be in breach of your contract.

EMPLOYMENT STATUS

The statutory rights you have depend on what your *employment status* is, as many statutory rights apply only if you are an *employee*, rather than *self-employed* or a *worker*:

- *Employees* work under a contract of employment. See below for factors to be taken into consideration to decide if someone is an employee or not. Examples of rights that only apply to employees are the rights to claim unfair dismissal, statutory redundancy pay, or statutory sick pay.

- *Workers* work under a contract of employment or a contract to personally perform work or services for a party who is not a client or a customer. The definition of workers includes all employees, but also includes casual workers, contract workers and agency workers, when they are not employees. Rights that extend to all workers include protection from discrimination, and the rights to paid holiday and minimum rest periods under the Working Time Regulations.

- *Self-employed people* work under a contract for services. People who are genuinely self-employed do not have many employment rights. One exception is the legislation providing protection against discrimination, which extends to self-employed people, as well as to employees and workers.

It is therefore important to know which category you fall into, as your employment status determines what employment protection you have.

It is not always obvious whether you are an employee, a worker, or self-employed, as there is no precise legal definition of what is required for someone to be an employee. You may have a contract stating that you are an employee, or it could expressly state that no relationship of employer/employee is formed and that you are self-employed. The terms of your contract are not conclusive evidence of your status; it could be that your legal status is the opposite of what it says in your contract. It will all depend on the reality of the situation, taking into account all the relevant factors. Similarly, you may be responsible for paying your own tax and National Insurance but this would not necessarily mean that you are genuinely self-employed.

A number of factors must be taken into account to determine your employment status, including the following:

- Control: how much control does the employer have over how, when and where you do the work? If you can send someone else to do the work in your place, it would suggest that you are self-employed, rather than an employee. For example, if a decorator can send someone else to do some painting, under their instruction, this would suggest they are self-employed, rather than employed by the person they are doing the painting for.

- Mutual obligation: is there any mutual obligation between you and the employer? Do they have an obligation to provide you with work, and do you have an obligation to carry out that work? For example, volunteers will very rarely be found to be employees, as there is usually no contractual obligation for the volunteer to carry out the work, or for the organisation to provide work for them to do.

- Economic reality: this means looking at the degree of financial risk that you have taken on in doing the work and the amount of capital you have invested, for example in buying equipment.

If you work through an employment agency, the question of your employment status could be complex. You could be an employee of the business that you are placed to work at, or possibly of the agency, or you could be a worker or self-employed, rather than an employee, and therefore have less employment protection. Your status will depend on the factors discussed above, such as who controls how, when and where you work, and whether there is any obligation for you to be provided with work, or for you to do the work. If you are uncertain about your rights as an agency worker, you should seek legal advice.

If a tribunal is required to decide what your employment status is, for example to establish whether you are entitled to a redundancy payment, or have the right to claim unfair dismissal, they will examine the situation considering all of the above factors, and make a decision based on the reality of the relationship.

DISCRIMINATION

The new law on age discrimination – the Employment Equality (Age) Regulations – was looked at in detail in chapter 1. Much of that law is based on previous discrimination legislation covering sex, race, disability, sexual orientation, and religion or belief, which means that in general the principles are the same in each category. As with age discrimination, the law defines the different forms that discrimination at work can come in (see the boxed text for these definitions). This section looks at details of each of these categories of discrimination, the differences between them and particular exemptions from the general principles.

TYPES OF DISCRIMINATION

Direct discrimination: treating someone less favourably than another person would be treated, because of their age, sex, race, disability, sexual orientation, or religion or belief.

Age is the only category in which direct discrimination can be justifiable.

Indirect discrimination: a policy or practice which puts people of a certain age group, sex, race, sexual orientation, or religion or belief at a disadvantage, compared with others.

Indirect discrimination can be justified if the employer can show it is necessary to achieve a legitimate business aim. Note that the law on disability discrimination does not use the concept of indirect discrimination (see below for more details).

Harassment: behaviour which creates an intimidating, hostile or offensive environment for a person to work in, for one of the above reasons (age, sex, race, etc).

Victimisation: putting someone at a disadvantage because they have made a complaint about discrimination, or have given information about someone else's complaint. You are also protected from victimisation if your employer thinks you are about to make a complaint, even if you have not yet done so.

Sex discrimination

The law on sex discrimination is found in the Sex Discrimination Act 1975 (as amended by later legislation). Direct discrimination is unlawful, so no employer could, for example, refuse to promote a woman to a senior position because they think women don't make good managers.

Unlike the age discrimination regulations, *direct discrimination on grounds of sex* cannot be justified by an employer. It will only be lawful to require a worker to be of a particular sex if the employer can show that this is a genuine occupational requirement for the position and this is only possible in limited circumstances set out in the Sex Discrimination Act. One example is for a dramatic performance where an actor of a particular sex is required, in the same way that actors of a particular age can be required under the age discrimination regulations. Decency and privacy are also reasons why you might employ someone of a particular sex; or if they will be providing personal services, such as those provided by a care assistant in some situations. It cannot be a genuine occupational requirement for the position holder to be a man if this is based solely on the need for physical strength to do the job. So an employer cannot advertise only for men when a physically strong woman would be equally able to do the job.

Indirect discrimination on the grounds of sex is unlawful but, as with age discrimination, it can sometimes be justified by the employer. To show indirect discrimination has taken place, you have to show that an employer has a policy or practice which puts women at a particular disadvantage compared with men (or vice versa). Cases brought under the Sex Discrimination Act for indirect discrimination are often based on the fact that a greater proportion of women than men have primary responsibility for childcare. This means that they are more likely to work part time, to have had breaks in their careers, or to have started their careers later than men. To succeed with an argument such as this, you may need statistical evidence to show that women in general are disproportionately affected. For example, if an employer making redundancies selects all part-time workers to be made redundant, this is likely to be indirect discrimination against women. In many cases of indirect discrimination you would need statistics to show that one group (in this example, women) is particularly disadvantaged, but it has been accepted by employment tribunals as common knowledge that more women than men work part time, and so statistical evidence is not required in each case based on this argument. The employer in this example may have had no intention to discriminate against their female employees but this would be irrelevant.

There can sometimes be an element of age discrimination in sex discrimination claims, and vice versa. For example, an upper age limit of 35 for a position would be direct age discrimination, but also possibly indirect sex discrimination, on the grounds that more women than men aged under 35 do not work because they are bringing up children. Another example could be the example given above of the employer making all part-time workers redundant. This would be indirect sex discrimination, as mentioned above, but it could also be indirect age discrimination if it could be shown that more older people than younger people work part time. (In this example the part-time employees would also have protection under the part-time workers regulations; see below for details.)

If you think you may have a claim for age discrimination, you should consider whether there may also be an element of sex discrimination involved.

The Act also covers sexual harassment. The definition of sexual harassment is *unwanted conduct on the grounds of a person's sex, or of a sexual nature, which has the purpose or effect of violating the person's dignity, or of creating an intimidating, hostile, degrading, humiliating or offensive environment for that person.* This definition will cover a situation where, for example, a woman doing a traditionally male-dominated job such as construction is bullied or ostracised by colleagues who don't believe a woman could or should be doing the job. It will also cover the situation where the harassment is of a sexual nature, either physically or verbally.

The protection of the Sex Discrimination Act also covers people who are discriminated against on the grounds of their marital status. Since December 2005, gay and lesbian couples who form a civil partnership also have the right not to be discriminated against on the grounds that they are in a civil partnership.

The law also protects transsexuals from discrimination on the grounds that they have undergone, or are undergoing, gender reassignment.

Most cases under the Act are taken by women claiming they are treated less favourably than a man would be in a comparable position, but men have the same rights as women under the Act, and can also claim that they have been discriminated against on the grounds of their gender.

Although it would seem logical for the Act to cover issues such as equal salaries for men and women, there is actually another Act that deals with this: the Equal Pay Act 1970. This covers your salary, occupational pension, and contractual benefits such as access to private health insurance. It is unlawful to pay men and women at different rates if they are doing work of equal value, unless there is another genuine reason for the difference.

Race discrimination
Legislation on race was the first anti-discrimination law in the UK, and came about with the first Race Relations Act in 1965. The law on race discrimination is now found in the Race Relations Act 1976, which has been amended on a number of occasions since it came into force. The main premise is, of course, that it is unlawful to discriminate against someone on racial grounds. This covers a person's colour, race, nationality or ethnic or national origins.

It is also unlawful to discriminate against someone on the grounds of their association with someone of a particular race: for example, if you are not invited to company functions because your partner is black.

As with direct sex discrimination, direct discrimination on the grounds of race cannot be justified and will be unlawful, unless it falls under the genuine occupational requirement exemption. The Race Relations Act sets out the following circumstances when this could be the case. It could be a genuine occupational requirement for an actor or model to be of a particular race; or for waiting staff in a restaurant where authenticity requires them to be of a particular race; or where the job is to provide welfare services to a particular racial group, it could be a requirement that the employee belong to that group.

As with the other discrimination laws, indirect discrimination on the grounds of race can be justified by an employer if they can show that the discrimination is a 'proportionate means of achieving a legitimate aim'. For example, a requirement for employees to be able to speak and write English to a high standard could indirectly discriminate against people who do not have English as a first language, but could be justified if it is necessary to be able to do the job.

Disability discrimination

To be protected under the Disability Discrimination Act 1995 you have to show that you fall within the definition of disability. This means that you have a physical or mental impairment which has a substantial and long-term adverse effect on your ability to carry out normal day-to-day activities. Normal day-to-day activities mean things like getting dressed, cooking, walking, sitting down, lifting things, shopping, or using public transport.

As with the other types of discrimination, direct disability discrimination is unlawful, as are victimisation and harassment. But there are other types of disability discrimination which are not found in the laws in other categories: disability-related discrimination, and the failure to comply with a duty to make reasonable adjustments. The concept of indirect discrimination is not used in relation to disability.

Disability-related discrimination happens when a disabled person is treated less favourably than another person would have been treated because of a reason related to their disability. An example of a disability-related reason would be if a partially sighted person is dismissed because they are unable to use a normal computer monitor; the reason for the dismissal would be that they cannot use the monitor, not the fact that they are partially sighted.

Disability-related discrimination is unlawful, unless the employer can justify it. When considering whether disability-related discrimination is justified, an employer must always consider whether there is any adjustment that could reasonably be made to prevent the person being at a disadvantage. A reasonable adjustment could be a physical alteration to the workplace, such as provision of a computer monitor suitable for a partially sighted person (as in the above example); or it could be an adjustment to the method or pattern of working, such as a change in hours or place of work. If an employer fails to make a reasonable adjustment which would prevent a disabled person from being at a disadvantage compared with a person without that disability, it will be unlawful discrimination.

For more detailed information on the Disability Discrimination Act, see chapter 14.

Sexual orientation discrimination

Sexual orientation, like age, is a latecomer to discrimination legislation; it was only made unlawful to discriminate on these grounds in December 2003. If you face discrimination or harassment from your employer or colleagues on the grounds of your sexual orientation, whether you are gay, lesbian, bisexual or heterosexual, you can make a claim under the Employment Equality (Sexual Orientation) Regulations 2003.

There is a noteworthy exemption under the law for employment for the purposes of an organised religion. If the 'doctrines of the religion' require it, an employer can refuse to hire someone of a particular sexual orientation if the employment is 'for the purposes of organised religion'. The courts have said that this exemption will only apply in very limited circumstances, such as the employment of priests or imams. So teachers in faith schools should not be discriminated against on the grounds of their sexuality.

Employees who are part of a gay or lesbian couple have the right to have the same employment benefits as employees who are part of a heterosexual couple. For example, if opposite-sex partners of staff of a transport company are entitled to free travel passes, same-sex partners must have the same benefits.

Religion or belief

The law against discrimination on the grounds of religion or belief was also introduced in December 2003. The Race Relations Act 1976 did not cover people of all religions, as it was necessary to show that people of the religion were members of a distinct racial group with a shared history and culture. So Sikhs and Jews were successful in bringing claims under the Act, as they were seen to have their own ethnic identity, but Muslims could not use the race law, as they are a racially mixed group.

Since 2003, you can take action against discrimination or harassment at work on the grounds of your religion or belief.

A possible example of indirect discrimination on the grounds of religion is where an employer imposes a dress code which bans all headwear. Fewer people of particular religions – for example, Sikhs or Muslim women, who keep their heads covered – would be able to comply with this. The employer may be able to justify the indirect discrimination, in which case it would be lawful.

Other areas

The law protects people from discrimination in a number of other areas too. It is unlawful to treat people less favourably on the grounds that they work part time or on a fixed-term contract, or because they are involved in union activity or are a 'whistle-blower'. The law in these areas is similar to those described above, although they are not usually thought of as being part of discrimination law.

Part-time work If you work part time, you are entitled to the same terms and conditions – on a pro rata basis if this is appropriate – as someone doing the same work on a full-time basis. Under the Part-time Workers Regulations 2000 you have the right not to be at a disadvantage because of your part-time status.

You're also entitled to the same hourly pay, the same access to the company pension scheme, the same annual leave (on a pro rata basis) and the same contractual sick pay as a comparable full-time worker.

This law applies to 'workers' rather than just to 'employees' (see the explanation on p. 19), and so casual and temporary workers are also protected. Women may also have a claim for indirect sex discrimination if they are treated less favourably because they work part time. This is because more women than men work part time and so they are more likely to be disadvantaged.

Fixed-term contracts If you are on a fixed-term contract, you have the right not to be treated less favourably than a permanent employee, unless the employer can justify this. This means that your terms and conditions should not be worse than those of a permanent employee doing comparable work.

Union activity You have the right not to be discriminated against on the grounds that you are a member of a trade union. If you are dismissed because you are a member of a union, or you have taken part in union activities, the dismissal will be automatically unfair.

Similarly, you have protection from discrimination on the grounds that you are *not* a union member.

If you are a union representative in a union recognised by your employer, you have the right to paid time off to carry out your union duties, such as attending meetings or training, or accompanying a colleague to a disciplinary meeting.

Whistle-blowing Under the Public Interest Disclosure Act 1998, workers have protection against being dismissed or suffering a detriment as a result of making certain types of complaint, or disclosing information in the public interest. You are protected by this law if you report some kind of activity on the part of your employer or colleagues, which you believe to be unlawful or dangerous. This could be either by making a complaint within the organisation, or by reporting it to an appropriate person outside (eg, a body such as the Environment Agency or the **Health and Safety Executive**). The kind of allegation that would be covered includes a report of a criminal act, a health and safety breach, or an act of environmental damage.

If you are dismissed because you have reported this kind of activity, the dismissal will be automatically unfair and you should make a claim to the employment tribunal. You can also claim compensation if you have not been dismissed but have suffered a detriment such as being demoted.

TERMS AND CONDITIONS OF EMPLOYMENT

Terms and conditions relating to pay are discussed in chapter 12.

Annual leave

All workers are entitled to a minimum of four weeks' paid holiday a year. This is the statutory minimum your employer must allow you to take, but if your contract provides for more than four weeks a year, that is the amount to which you are entitled. The statutory minimum four weeks can include bank holidays, but many employers will give you bank holidays off in addition to your normal annual leave. However, there is no statutory right to have bank holidays off and so your employer can actually require you to work these days without giving you time off in lieu.

If you work part time, your holiday should be calculated pro rata. So, for example, if you work two days a week, you would be entitled to a minimum of eight days' annual leave (that is, four two-day weeks).

You do *not* have the right to take your holiday whenever you choose. Your employer can insist that you take it at certain times. Quite often, employers ask their staff to take their holiday at the least busy times of the year, or at a different time to their colleagues. Your employer may allow you to carry some holiday over to the next year, although unless your contract gives you the right to do so, your employer will not be obliged to allow this. If your employer does not allow you to take all of your holiday entitlement in the relevant year, you should make a formal complaint, using your employer's grievance procedure. If this is not successful you can make a claim at an employment tribunal (for more information see chapter 5).

When you leave a job, you are entitled to be paid in lieu for any accrued annual leave that you have not taken. If you have taken more than the statutory minimum you were entitled to, on a pro rata basis, your employer can only make deductions from your wages to account for this if this is provided for in your contract, or if there is another written agreement which allows this. If you have been paid more than your contractual entitlement, your contract will probably include a term allowing your employer to deduct this from your final pay. Even if there is no express term allowing this, a tribunal can decide that this is an 'implied term' in the contract, and allow your employer to do this.

Working hours and breaks

The legislation that sets out how much holiday you are entitled to, the Working Time Regulations, also sets out minimum rest periods that you must be allowed. The maximum number of hours that any employer can require you to work is 48 hours a week. This is calculated on an average basis, usually over a period of 17 weeks, so there could be some weeks where you work more than 48 hours.

You can opt out of this 48-hour maximum if you choose to do so. To do this, you must sign an agreement with your employer, stating that you agree to work more than an average of 48 hours a week. Your employer cannot force you to sign the opt-out agreement. If you are dismissed or suffer a disadvantage at work because you refuse to opt out, this will be an unfair dismissal.

You also have the right to at least 11 consecutive hours' rest from work a day, and at least one day off a week. If your working day lasts more than six hours, you are entitled to at least one rest break of 20 minutes a day, although this time off does not have to be paid.

Of course, many people regularly work longer hours with fewer breaks than they are legally entitled to. There is often a culture of long hours in certain work areas, and although you may choose to work in this way, it is worth remembering that the law is there to protect all workers from exploitation.

Notice periods

Once you have worked for the same employer for one month, you are entitled to a minimum of one week's notice of dismissal. This increases by one week for each full year of employment. So after you have worked for the same employer for two complete years, you are entitled to a minimum of two weeks' notice; then three weeks' notice after three years, and so on up to a maximum of 12 weeks' notice after 12 years. As with all statutory minimum rights, your contract can provide for more generous notice and your employer must stick to their contractual obligations.

If your employer does not give you the amount of notice required under your contract, you can claim *wrongful dismissal* at an employment tribunal. You would be entitled to compensation for the unpaid notice period. Wrongful dismissal is different from unfair dismissal: a wrongful dismissal is a dismissal which is in breach of the contract of employment; an unfair dismissal is a dismissal for which there was no fair reason, or which was procedurally unfair. For more details on unfair dismissal see chapter 3.

Your employer can give you pay in lieu of notice, rather than requiring you to work your notice period, as long as this is provided for in your contract. If your contract does not state that you can be paid in lieu of notice, it will be a breach of contract. However, it is usually not worth claiming wrongful dismissal, as you would not be entitled to any compensation on top of what you had already been paid in lieu of notice.

If you do something which is a serious breach of your contract, such as committing gross misconduct by coming into work drunk, or assaulting your manager, your employer can dismiss you without notice. As long as your employer was correct in treating your behaviour as a breach of contract, you will not succeed with a claim for wrongful dismissal and you will not be entitled to pay in lieu of notice.

Your contract will probably include a minimum period of notice that you must give your employer, if you decide to leave the job. If you leave without giving the minimum contractual notice required, your employer could sue you for breach of contract, claiming any losses they may have suffered as a result of having to replace you. If there is nothing specified in your contract then the minimum notice you must give is one week, regardless of how long you have worked for the employer.

Changing the terms of your contract

Your employer cannot change the terms of your contract unless you agree to the change, either on an individual basis or through a collective agreement made between your employer and employee representatives. So your employer cannot change your contractual hours, pay, entitlement to notice, holiday pay, etc without your agreement.

If they do attempt a unilateral change to an important term of your contract, you may have a claim for breach of contract. If you resign, or are dismissed for not accepting the change, you may also have a claim for unfair dismissal; however, there is no guarantee that this will succeed, as the employment tribunal could agree that the change was necessary for business reasons, and it was reasonable to dismiss you for not accepting it. If you claim unfair dismissal after resigning, you would argue that your employer's change in your contract amounted to a *constructive dismissal*. This means that your employer has acted in a way that is a breach of your contract, which brings your employment relationship to an end and entitles you to resign without giving notice. For more details of constructive dismissal, see page 37.

Examples of situations where you may be entitled to resign and claim constructive dismissal would be if your employer withholds your pay, or changes your terms of employment, without your agreement, so that you are earning significantly less, either because you are working fewer hours or because your pay has been reduced. To be eligible to claim unfair dismissal, whether it is a constructive dismissal or not, you must have worked for the same employer for at least one complete year.

If you are unhappy about a change in your contract, it is important that you do not continue working under the new terms without making it clear to your employer that you do not agree to them; otherwise you may seem to have accepted your employer's breach of contract and would lose your right to claim unfair dismissal.

Obviously, there are other factors to consider before resigning, such as the likelihood of finding a new job on better terms than your current employer is offering you. If you are in this situation, you should seek legal advice immediately, either from your union, if you are a member, or from **Citizens Advice**, a **Law Centre** or a solicitor (see details on p. 78).

Changing your place of work

If your employer asks you to work in a different location, this could be a breach of contract, depending on the circumstances. Your contract could include a mobility clause, which requires you to work on a different site if required, but even if this is the case, the employer has to behave reasonably in enforcing this contract term. For example, if you have always worked at the same site in Leeds, it would seem unreasonable for the employer to expect you to relocate to Plymouth with very little notice. This could be a breach of your contract, even if there is an express clause allowing a change of location.

If there is no clause in your contract stating that you can be required to work at a different location, it may well be a breach of contract if your employer requires you to move. Again, it will depend on the circumstances, such as the distance involved and the notice given. If the change does amount to a breach of contract, you could resign and claim constructive unfair dismissal. Again, if you are in this situation you should seek legal advice.

A requirement for employees to change their place of work could also amount to indirect discrimination. For example, more women may be unable to comply with the requirement than men, as it could affect their childcare responsibilities.

If your workplace is closing down, or relocating to a different site, you may be entitled to a redundancy payment. See chapter 3 for more details on redundancy.

The sale or transfer of the business

If your employer sells their business, or the part of the business that you work in, you have protection under the Transfer of Undertakings Regulations (TUPE). When the sale takes place, your contract of employment is transferred to the new owner, and you automatically become their employee. You have the right to keep the same terms and conditions of employment that you had under your old employer.

If you are dismissed – either by the original employer, or the new owner – because of the sale of the business, or if the new employer tries to change a fundamental term of your contract, it could be an unfair dismissal. If you are in this situation you should get legal advice, as the position can be complicated.

BULLYING

According to the Health and Safety Executive, 12.8 million working days were lost in 2004/05 due to stress, anxiety and depression. Often this is down to an excessive workload and a lack of adequate support, but it can also frequently result from difficult working relationships with colleagues or managers, either because of poor people-management skills on the part of managers, or because of intentional bullying. There is no specific legal protection against bullying at work but in some circumstances it may be possible to take action, either through a claim for constructive unfair dismissal or a personal injury claim, or by using discrimination law.

It is important to remember that legal action should usually be seen as a last resort. If you are being bullied, or if something else about your working conditions, such as a heavy workload, unjustified criticism, or lack of support, is causing you to suffer from stress or anxiety, you should try to resolve the matter informally and if that fails, make use of your employer's grievance procedure. This should be done as early as possible. If you are a member of a union, you should ask your union representative for help. If your employer has a human resources department, it may be that they can help you, even if you are not getting useful support from your line manager. See chapter 4 on alternative dispute resolution options.

Constructive unfair dismissal

If the situation becomes so serious that you feel you are unable to continue working, you may be able to resign and claim constructive unfair dismissal. See chapter 3.

In all but the most serious circumstances, an employment tribunal would expect you to have attempted to resolve the situation by lodging an official grievance with your employer. If you use your employer's grievance procedure but they do not deal with your complaint adequately, and your working life becomes unendurable, you may then be able to resign and claim constructive dismissal. You will need to show that your employer's failure to address your complaint is serious enough to be a breach of contract.

Personal injury

Your employer has a duty to make sure you have the support and equipment to enable you to do your job safely, and this includes protecting your emotional health and well-being, as well as your physical safety. If bullying at work causes you to become ill, you may be able to bring a claim for personal injury against your employer, but be warned: personal injury claims arising from work-related stress are rarely successful. You have to show that your employer should have foreseen that you would become ill and that they could have prevented it but failed to do so. For a court to find your employer liable in a personal injury claim, it is also necessary to prove that you have a clinically recognised psychological or psychiatric condition, as a result of your working conditions. It is not enough to have a diagnosis of 'stress'.

Therefore, for the many people suffering stress as a result of work, a personal injury claim is not an option in terms of obtaining redress from their employer.

Harassment

As discussed above, if you are being bullied on the grounds of age, sex, race, disability, sexual orientation, or religion or belief, you will have protection under the various anti-discrimination laws. Harassment claims can only be brought if the harassment is on one of these grounds, not if the bullying is for some other reason, or where there appears to be no particular reason.

Leaving Work Against Your Wishes

However carefully you plan your working life and eventual retirement, there is always a possibility that something will happen outside of your control.

There are a number of reasons you could be dismissed against your wishes; for example, redundancy, forced retirement, or reasons relating to your conduct or performance. If you are unfortunate enough to find yourself in a situation where you have been treated unfairly, there may be legal action you can take. This chapter sets out the legal position on dismissal, including the new law on retirement, and describes the procedural requirements for employers to follow when dismissing for any reason. For information on how to enforce your legal rights see chapter 5.

RETIREMENT AGAINST YOUR WISHES

A major part of the new law outlawing age discrimination deals with new procedures surrounding retirement. Until this new law, employers could force an employee to retire at any age they chose, which has sometimes led to people being forced out of work well before they felt ready to stop, and when they were more than capable of carrying on.

SUMMARY OF THE RETIREMENT PROCEDURE

1 The employer must give the employee six to twelve months' notice, both of the date of retirement and of the employee's right to request to continue working.

2 If the employee wishes to make a request to continue working, they must do so three to six months before the intended retirement date, in writing, stating that it is a request under Paragraph 5 of Schedule 6 to the regulations, and stating whether they wish to continue working indefinitely, for a stated period, or until a stated date.

3 The employer must hold a meeting with the employee, within a reasonable period of time, to discuss the request. The employee has a right to be accompanied by a colleague of their choice.

4 As soon as is reasonably practicable, the employer must give the employee notice of their decision. If they have agreed to the request, they must confirm whether employment will continue indefinitely, or for a certain period. If the request has been refused, they must confirm the intended date of retirement.

5 If the request is refused, or the employer agrees to continued employment for a shorter period than was requested by the employee, the employee has the right to an appeal meeting. The employer must inform the employee of this right when notice of the original decision is given.

6 If the employee requests an appeal, they must do so as soon as reasonably practicable after notice of the employer's decision, setting out the grounds of the appeal. The employer must arrange a meeting within a reasonable period. Again, the employee has a right to be accompanied by a colleague of their choice.

7   As soon as is reasonably practicable after the appeal meeting, the employer must give notice of their decision, giving details as in step 4 above.

There is some evidence that businesses are starting to come around to the idea that flexible retirement policies make economic sense and that dismissing a capable, productive, experienced employee just because they have reached a certain birthday does not benefit the business. We hear a lot about the ageing population and potential future skills shortage caused by fewer younger workers. Many larger employers are waking up to this and are looking at ways of retaining their older workers in order to avoid problems in the future. This is good news for those who wish to remain in work, whether for economic or personal reasons.

Of course, many people would prefer to retire as soon as possible. The new law is not designed to force you to continue working when this is not your choice and it will not affect voluntary retirements to which both you and your employer agree. It is aimed at protecting you from being forced to retire when you wish to continue working, or when your pension provision does not allow you to retire on a comfortable income.

When talking about retirement, it is important to remember the difference between retirement age and pension age. There is no national retirement age – although the new age regulations introduce what is known as a 'default retirement age' – but there is a state pension age, which is currently 60 for women and 65 for men (this will level up to 65 for both between 2010 and 2020). You can draw your state pension at this age, but *you do not have to retire*. State pension age will not be affected by the age regulations. For more information on state pensions, including deferring your pension, see chapter 13.

RETIREMENT PROCEDURE – WHEN IS FORCED RETIREMENT LEGAL?

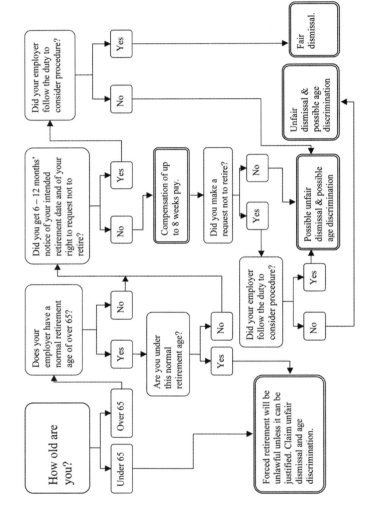

The *default retirement age* is set at 65. This is the same for both men and women. The default retirement age means that below age 65, employers will have to be able to justify forcing someone to retire, whereas over 65, justification is not needed and it will be lawful as long as the proper procedures are carried out. Employers will not *have* to retire people at this age; in fact they have a duty to consider an employee's request to continue working.

So the age regulations give people under 65 protection they previously did not have; it is now only lawful to force people below 65 to retire in exceptional circumstances, when retirement at this age can be justified by the employer. However, the protection against enforced retirement for people over age 65 is very limited.

RETIREMENT UNDER 65

If your employer tries to force you to retire under the default retirement age of 65, this will be unlawful age discrimination, unless they can show that the retirement age is justified. It is likely that it will be very difficult for employers to justify a retirement age under 65, but this will be up to the employment tribunal to decide in each case. A retirement under age 65 which is not justified will also be an unfair dismissal.

RETIREMENT OVER 65

If you are over 65, have reached your employer's *normal retirement age* (if they have one) and all the correct procedures have been followed, then you can be forced into retirement. For this to be fair you must be given between six and twelve months' notice of both your retirement date and your right to request to continue working. If you make a request to continue, then your employer must follow the correct procedures.

Before the new law came into force, around one third of employers had a compulsory retirement age. Under the new law, employers who set their retirement age at under 65 will either have to change this or justify it. Most employers already work on a more flexible basis when it comes to retiring employees. There may be a retirement age specified in your contract, but if in practice employees doing your job within the same organisation usually retire at a different age, then this will be the normal retirement age, for the purposes of the law, not that set in the contract.

The right to request not to retire

This is a new right for employees to make a request not to retire on the date the employer has proposed. The employer has a duty to consider a request if you make one, as long as it was made within the time limits set by the law. Your employer must give you notice of your right to make a request between six and twelve months before the retirement date. You must make your request at least three months before the retirement date. Strangely, you cannot make the request more than six months before the retirement date, even if you have been given the maximum 12 months' notice. When you make your request you should state whether you want to continue working indefinitely, for a certain period, or until a certain date. Your request must be in writing and you should state clearly that you are making a request not to retire under paragraph 5 of Schedule 6 to the Employment Equality (Age) Regulations 2006. You can base your request letter on the sample on page 45.

There are certain steps that your employer must then follow, known as 'the duty to consider procedure', for the retirement to be a fair dismissal. They must hold a meeting with you, within a reasonable period of time, to discuss your request. You have a right to be accompanied at the meeting by a colleague; this can be a union representative but only if they also work for the same employer. Your employer must then tell you their decision

Date

Dear .....

I am writing to request not to retire on your intended date of [insert employer's intended date of retirement]. I am making this request under paragraph 5 of Schedule 6 to the Employment Equality (Age) Regulations 2006.

I propose that my employment should continue [you must specify one of the following:]

• indefinitely

• for [insert a specific period, eg 12 months]

• until [insert a specific date].

[If you wish to, you can include information in support of your request, such as examples of how allowing you to continue working could benefit the organisation.]

I look forward to hearing from you with your suggested time for a meeting to discuss my request.

Yours sincerely

. . . .

as soon as is reasonably practicable after the meeting. If you are not happy with the decision – for example, if your request to stay on has been refused completely or your employer has agreed to let you continue working for a shorter period than you requested – you have the right to an appeal meeting with your employer.

There is no requirement for your employer to give you a reason for their decision and so although you have the right to an appeal meeting you may have little more to add to what you said at the first meeting, as you may not know why your request has been refused. In the original draft of the regulations, there was a requirement for the employer to consider the request 'in good faith', but this was not included in the final version. It will only be possible to challenge your employer's decision on the grounds that they have not followed the correct procedure – for example if you are denied an appeal meeting – not on the grounds that the decision was unfair, or that it was based on factually incorrect information, or that your employer did not give genuine consideration to your request.

Compensation when your employer does not follow the rules

If your employer does not follow the new rules on retirement, there are three different ways you can claim compensation:

1 You may be able to claim compensation for receiving *less than six months' notice.*

2 You may have a claim for *unfair dismissal,* if your employer has not followed the correct procedure, or retirement is not the real reason for your dismissal.

3 You may have a claim for *age discrimination,* if they try to retire you before age 65, or before their normal retirement age, and cannot justify doing so; or if you are dismissed at any age when retirement is not the real reason.

Your employer is required to give you at least six months' notice of your retirement date and of your right to request not to retire. If you are given less than six months' notice of either your retirement date or of your right to request not to retire, you can claim compensation at the employment tribunal of up to eight weeks' pay. The value of a week's pay is currently capped at

£290 and so the maximum compensation would be £2,320 (this cap is usually increased every February).

This compensation is in addition to any you would be awarded if the retirement is also found to be an unfair dismissal or age discrimination.

When forced retirement will be an unfair dismissal

If your employer attempts to retire you with less than two weeks' notice, or gives you less than two weeks' notice of your right to request not to retire, it counts automatically as an unfair dismissal. The thinking behind this is that, if it was a genuine retirement, your employer should have been in a position to give you more notice: less than two weeks' notice is clearly not enough time to allow the employee to make plans for their retirement. In this situation you should start a claim at the tribunal, within three months of the date of the dismissal, for age discrimination, unfair dismissal and the maximum eight weeks' compensation for getting less than six months' notice.

As there is no longer an upper age limit to the right to claim unfair dismissal (see below), employers can no longer dismiss someone over age 65 without having a fair reason, as they could in the past. This means that some employers may try to use retirement to cover up another reason for dismissal; for example to avoid having to go through disciplinary procedures if the reason for the dismissal is the employee's conduct or performance. There is also a risk that an employer could try to 'retire' an employee in order to avoid having to pay a redundancy payment, where the real reason for the dismissal is redundancy.

If you are given at least six months' notice, the tribunal will automatically accept that retirement is the real reason for the dismissal, and will not consider alternatives (even if there is evidence of another reason such as redundancy). In this situation it will be a fair dismissal, as long as the correct procedure is followed. If you get less than two weeks' notice it will automatically be an unfair dismissal; however, if your employer gives you somewhere between six months' and two weeks' notice, the situation is less clear. In these circumstances it would be for the tribunal to decide whether retirement was the real reason for the dismissal. If they decide your employer was really dismissing you for another reason, it will be an unfair dismissal. When deciding what the reason was for your dismissal, the tribunal will consider how much notice you have been given and whether your employer has made an attempt to follow the duty to consider procedure. The less notice you have been given, the less likely it is that they will accept that it was a genuine retirement.

In all cases, if your employer fails to follow the 'duty to consider procedure' (holding a meeting to discuss your request to stay on, then informing you of their decision and giving you the right to appeal) the dismissal will be unfair. See below for details on compensation for unfair dismissal claims, and chapter 5 on how to bring a claim at the tribunal.

Effectively, if you are over age 65, you can still be forced into retirement with very little notice and limited compensation. In theory it's possible that you could be given just over two weeks' notice and the dismissal would be seen to be fair, although you would be able to claim up to eight weeks' compensation and your employer would have to consider your request to stay on. This is clearly not enough time to adjust to a major life change such as retirement. The importance of planning ahead for retirement is discussed in chapter 11.

UNFAIR DISMISSAL

Dismissals in the context of retirement are dealt with above. This section looks at the fairness of dismissals for all other reasons. Your dismissal could be unfair either because your employer did not have a fair reason, or because they followed an unfair procedure in dismissing you.

The age discrimination regulations removed the upper age limit for unfair dismissal claims. Before the new law, if you were over your employer's normal retirement age, or over 65 if they had no normal retirement age, you could not claim unfair dismissal. This meant that if you had a new boss who didn't get on with you, they could dismiss you, with no explanation, as long as there was no evidence of discrimination. (The only situation where there was no upper age limit for unfair dismissal was if you were dismissed for one of the limited number of automatically unfair reasons, such as being involved in trade union activities or for complaining about breaches of health and safety. See p. 52.)

People of all ages now have the right to claim unfair dismissal, but there are still other eligibility requirements, other than age, for making a claim. You can only claim unfair dismissal if you are an employee. It is sometimes unclear as to whether you are an employee or not, for example if you are working for an agency (see pp. 97–8). Also, you can only claim unfair dismissal if you have been working for the same employer for at least one year. There is little protection against dismissal for people in their first year of employment; the only exception to the requirement for one year's service is for automatically unfair dismissals, which are looked at on page 52.

WRITTEN REASONS FOR DISMISSAL

As long as you have worked for your employer for at least one year, you are entitled to written reasons for your dismissal. You should write to your employer asking for this. If your employer does not give you the reason in writing within two weeks of your request, or you think the reason they have given is not true, you have the right to apply to a tribunal for compensation of up to two weeks' pay. This would be in addition to any compensation you are entitled to if the dismissal is found to be unfair. The tribunal can also decide what the real reason was for your dismissal.

If your employer has followed the statutory disciplinary and dismissal procedure, you should have already been notified of the reason they were considering dismissing you, before you were actually dismissed. See below for more details on this procedure.

Before making a claim for unfair dismissal at an employment tribunal, you should consider whether there is any other way you can try to resolve things with your employer (see chapters 4 and 5 for more information on dispute resolution). For example, if your employer has used the proper procedure, you should have been given the opportunity to appeal against the decision to dismiss you. You should usually make sure you have exhausted the appeals procedure before making your application to the tribunal, but remember there is a time limit of three months from the date you were dismissed and, even if the appeals process is ongoing, you must get your application to the tribunal before the end of these three months.

If you do make a claim for unfair dismissal, the tribunal will look at two aspects when deciding whether the dismissal was fair or not. First they will look at whether your employer had a fair reason for dismissing you, and second they will look at whether your employer acted reasonably in dismissing you for that reason, including whether they followed a fair procedure when making the decision to dismiss you.

Your employer will have to show the tribunal that they had a fair reason for dismissing you. This might be your conduct or capability, or it may be your job is redundant. There may be other reasons which your employer could persuade the tribunal are fair.

If you think that the real reason for your dismissal is your age, you can claim both age discrimination and unfair dismissal. It can be difficult to prove this at the employment tribunal as it is unlikely that your employer will admit to discriminating against you on the grounds of your age. However, there may be evidence to *suggest* that this was the real reason and if you can establish that age *could* have been the reason, it will then be up to your employer to prove that this was not the case.

Conduct If your employer is dismissing you for reasons connected to your conduct, they do not have to have conclusive proof that you have done whatever it is they are dismissing you for. They only have to have a genuine reasonable belief that you have behaved in that way, following a reasonable investigation into the matter. For example, an employer may have dismissed an employee for stealing stock. They would not need to have proof that the employee had done it, to the same standard as say a criminal court would need for a conviction. The employer has to carry out a reasonable investigation which may include interviewing any witnesses, and should include asking the employee for their side of the story. However, as long as it is reasonable on the evidence they have for them to conclude that the employee did steal, it would be fair for them to dismiss that employee, provided they follow all the correct procedures. If the employee then claimed unfair dismissal, they would lose the claim, even if evidence came to light at the tribunal which proved that they had not done what they were accused of. It is the employer's knowledge and belief at the time they decide to dismiss you that is relevant, not what is found out at a later stage.

Capability If your employer is dismissing you because of your performance or capability in your job, they would be expected to have given you support and assistance to improve your performance, before dismissing you. This may involve giving you extra training or coaching and increased monitoring of your work. Particular problems with your performance should be brought to your attention and you should be given a chance to improve before being dismissed.

Health It can sometimes be fair for your employer to dismiss you because of health problems. Your employer has a responsibility to investigate the situation, including discussing it with you, and possibly obtaining information from your doctor, to find out if you will be able to continue working. They would also be expected to consider whether there is any alternative work you could do, or any adjustments that could be made to allow you to continue working.

If you are absent from work for a long period for health reasons, and there is little realistic prospect of your health improving so that you can return to work, your employer would almost certainly be justified in dismissing you, as long as they have followed the dismissal procedure fairly. If you are disabled, within the meaning of the Disability Discrimination Act, you have additional protection against discrimination on the grounds of your disability. See chapters 2 and 14 for information on disability discrimination.

Automatically unfair dismissal Some reasons for dismissal will be automatically unfair, for example if your employer dismisses you because you have taken part in trade union activities, because you have reported a breach of health and safety, or because you have tried to assert a right such as being paid the national minimum wage, or taking time off to deal with an emergency involving a dependent relative. If the tribunal accepts that the dismissal was for one of these reasons, they will not go on to consider whether the employer was reasonable or whether a correct procedure was followed; they will automatically decide that the dismissal was unfair.

Disciplinary and dismissal procedures

Unless your dismissal was for one of the automatically unfair reasons, the tribunal will look at whether it was procedurally fair. Since 2004, employers have been required by law to have a disciplinary procedure which they should follow if they are considering disciplining or dismissing an employee. The law aets down a minimum basic procedure but some employers will have their own more detailed procedure which may include extra steps and requirements; if they do, you should make sure that they are following that. The minimum basic procedure is set out here.

1 Your employer must write to you setting out details of the reasons they are considering disciplining or dismissing you.

2 A meeting must be held to discuss this.

3 You must be given the right to have an appeal meeting.

If your employer has not followed this minimum procedure your dismissal will be unfair, even if the reason for the dismissal was fair.

Even if your employer does follow this minimum procedure, your dismissal may still be unfair if the tribunal decides that your employer was unreasonable to dismiss you for the reason they did, or because in some other way the dismissal was procedurally unfair. For example, in a large organisation, if a manager has made serious allegations about your conduct and is the only alleged witness, a tribunal could find that it was an unfair dismissal if the same manager conducted the investigation and made the decision to dismiss you.

The only time when an employer would not be expected to carry out the full disciplinary procedure is in a situation of gross misconduct. Gross misconduct is conduct which is so bad it justifies immediate dismissal without notice. For example, if a manager sees an employee being violent towards a customer, that manager would almost certainly be justified in dismissing the employee for gross misconduct. However, even in this situation, your employer must still write to you with the reasons for your dismissal and give you the right to appeal against the decision.

Constructive dismissal

It is sometimes possible to claim unfair dismissal, even if you have resigned rather than been dismissed. This is called constructive dismissal. You have to show that your employer had treated you so badly that it amounted to a fundamental breach of your contract and you could not carry on working for them. If there has been a breach of your contract, you are entitled to resign without notice and claim unfair dismissal (as long as you meet the relevant eligibility requirements for unfair dismissal, see page 49). It is important that you act quickly as, if you wait too long before resigning, you could be seen to have accepted your employer's conduct. Constructive dismissal claims are complicated and, if you feel you are in this situation, you should seek legal advice immediately (see p. 34 for details).

If you are the victim of harassment either from colleagues or management, this could amount to constructive dismissal, depending on the seriousness of the situation. See chapter 1 (p. 6) for an explanation of the legal meaning of harassment.

It can also be a constructive dismissal if your employer tries to change the terms of your contract without your agreement. See chapter 2 (pp. 34–35) for more information on this.

Wrongful dismissal

Wrongful dismissal is a dismissal which is a breach of your contract. The most common example of wrongful dismissal is if your employer gives you less notice than is required by your contract. You can claim compensation for losses resulting from the wrongful dismissal; usually this will be the amount you would have been paid if you had been given the correct notice.

Compensation for unfair dismissal

If you win a claim of unfair dismissal, the tribunal can either order your employer to give you your job back, or can order your employer to pay you compensation. An order for compensation is much more common than reinstatement in your job.

An award for compensation will come in two parts. First, there is a basic award linked to your length of service. This is calculated in the same way as a statutory redundancy payment and the maximum at the time of writing is £8,700. Second, there is a compensatory award which is based on your losses and future losses from being dismissed, for example loss of earnings. This part of the award is currently capped at £58,400.

If you have also been successful with a claim for age discrimination, for example if the tribunal decided the real reason for your dismissal was your age, you can be awarded compensation for this, including compensation for what is known as 'injury to feelings'. Unlike unfair dismissal, the maximum compensation for discrimination claims is unlimited.

REDUNDANCY

Some people think of redundancy as a golden opportunity, if they've been thinking of making a change anyway and the company is offering generous terms for those who are selected or who put themselves forward.

For others it can be a very tough experience, depriving them of friends, colleagues and a job they're happy in, and forcing them back into a competitive marketplace they may not feel equipped to deal with.

In an ideal world, an employer should handle the situation with sympathy and sensitivity. Even if this isn't the case they must follow the correct procedures, which are designed to afford a basic level of protection to those being made redundant.

Whatever the circumstances, you may find yourself in need of advice, support or training to help you cope with an unexpected redundancy. There is further information for people who have recently left work in chapters 6, 7 and 8.

People sometimes refer to 'being made redundant' to mean 'being dismissed', when actually redundancy is not the real reason for the dismissal. There is a very specific legal definition of redundancy and if you are told that you are being made redundant, you should think about whether it really is a redundancy, or whether perhaps you are being dismissed unfairly, for some other reason.

Your job will be redundant if any of the following situations applies:

1 The business closes down entirely.

2 The business closes down in the place where you work.

3 There is no longer a need for the type of work you do (either just in your workplace or in the organisation in general).

4 Fewer people are needed to do the type of work you do (either in your workplace or in the organisation in general).

If you are told that you are being made redundant, but you do not think that any of these situations applies, you may be able to claim unfair dismissal (see pp. 47 ff.). If an employment tribunal finds that you have been unfairly dismissed, you will be entitled to compensation, which could be more than you would receive as a redundancy payment.

A dismissal which your employer says is for redundancy could be unfair, either because your job is not really redundant and your employer did not have another fair reason for dismissing you, or because the employer has not followed the correct procedure in carrying out the redundancies.

Selection for redundancy

If it is not the whole workforce that is being made redundant, the employer has to decide which employees are to be selected for redundancy. The employer must be careful to make this selection fairly, on the grounds of objective factors, such as each employee's productivity, skills, attendance record, or ability to meet the specific needs of the employer.

Following the introduction of the age discrimination regulations, it is no longer lawful for employers to select people on grounds of age. This behaviour would now qualify as unlawful age discrimination – unless the employer can justify this policy (see pp. 4–6) – and also unfair dismissal. It would probably also be unlawful age discrimination for employers to select people on the basis of their length of service, for example a policy of 'last in, first out' (known as LIFO) could indirectly discriminate against younger workers. When talking about age discrimination, it is important to remember that all discriminatory practices can potentially be justified by employers and so it is not possible to say that something will *definitely* be unlawful.

Similarly, if employers select for redundancy on the basis of productivity or levels of sickness absence there is a possibility that this would be disability-related discrimination. Again, it may be possible for an employer to justify these policies.

Consultation

Your employer has a duty to consult with you and your colleagues about the planned redundancies. This means they have to inform you of the need for redundancies as soon as possible, and discuss with you any alternative jobs that may be available within the organisation. If there is a recognised union where you work, the union should be involved in the consultation, but even if this is going on, your employer should also consult with you on an individual basis and this should be done before the notices of redundancies are given to individual employees. If 20 or more people are being made redundant, the employer must consult with the recognised trade union, or employee representatives if there is no union. Again, this must be done before individual employees are given notice of their redundancies.

If your employer has not consulted properly, you may have a claim for unfair dismissal. In addition to this, if your employer had a duty to consult with the union or employee representatives because 20 or more people were being made redundant, and they failed to do this properly, you could claim up to 90 days' pay if you were selected for redundancy. This is called a protective award. A claim for unfair dismissal and/or a protective award must be made to the employment tribunal within three months of the date of the dismissal.

As part of the consultation process, your employer has to consider whether there is any suitable alternative work you could do within the organisation. If you unreasonably refuse an offer of suitable alternative work, you can lose your entitlement to a redundancy payment. If you think you have been unfairly denied a redundancy payment on this basis, you should submit a claim to the employment tribunal. It would then be for the tribunal to decide whether the alternative job you were offered was in fact 'suitable' and whether you were 'unreasonable' in turning it down.

In addition to following the redundancy procedures as above, your employer also has to follow the normal dismissal and disciplinary procedure (see p. 52) before they dismiss you, even in a genuine redundancy situation. This involves writing to you to explain the reason that they are considering dismissing you, then holding a meeting with you to discuss this, and giving you the right to have an appeal meeting. If this procedure is not followed, your dismissal could be unfair, even if all of the other redundancy procedures are followed correctly.

Redundancy payments

If your dismissal is genuinely for reasons of redundancy and the selection and consultation procedure has been carried out fairly, you will have no grounds to challenge the decision. However, you will probably be entitled to compensation in the form of a redundancy payment, either the statutory minimum amount or the amount that is set out in your contract if this is more.

You will be entitled to the *statutory minimum redundancy payment* if you have been employed by the same employer for at least two years. Until 1 October 2006, you could only get a redundancy payment if you were aged under 65 but this upper age limit has been removed by the age discrimination regulations. The payment will still be calculated on the basis of your age and on your length of service, even though there are obvious elements of age discrimination against younger workers. The government has said that this approach is justified, as older workers will find it more difficult to get back into employment and therefore it is fair that they should be paid a higher redundancy payment in compensation.

STATUTORY REDUNDANCY PAYMENT CALCULATION

You are entitled to half a week's pay for every year you have worked for your employer when you were aged between 18 and 21, one week's pay for every year when you were aged between 22 and 40, and one and a half weeks' pay for every year when you were aged 40 or over. The amount of a week's pay is currently capped at £290 and the number of years taken into account is capped at 20. Therefore the maximum statutory redundancy payment is currently £8,700. The cap for a maximum week's pay is usually increased every February.

So, for example, if you are made redundant at age 60, having worked for your employer for 15 years, and your weekly wage is £350, you would be entitled to £6,525. This is 1.5 times your weekly pay capped at £290, multiplied by 15, the number of years of continuous employment. The multiplier is 1.5 because for all of those 15 years you were aged over 41.

You should be paid your redundancy payment as soon as you are made redundant, or soon afterwards. If you do not receive your payment, or you think you have not been paid enough, and you cannot resolve the problem with your employer, you can make a claim at the employment tribunal. A claim for a statutory redundancy payment must be submitted within six months of your dismissal.

Some employers pay more than the statutory minimum amount for a redundancy payment. This could be set out in your contract, or it may be negotiated through a union. If your contract states that you are entitled to more than the statutory minimum, then this is what your employer must pay you. If your employer refuses to pay redundancy pay you are entitled to under your contract, you can make a claim for breach of contract, either at the employment tribunal (where the time limit is three months), or at the county court (where the time limit is six years).

If you are made redundant because your employer is insolvent, they may not be able to pay you your redundancy payment. In this situation you can claim your statutory redundancy payment from the **Insolvency Service's Redundancy Payments Office**. You may also be able to claim any unpaid wages, holiday pay or notice pay through this office. You should complete form RP1 which is available from the Redundancy Payments Office either by downloading it at www.insolvency.gov.uk or by contacting their helpline on 0845 145 0004. This helpline can also give you further information about your entitlement to a redundancy payment.

Effect on benefits and tax If you are paid the minimum statutory redundancy payment, this will not affect your entitlement to benefits, although it will usually be treated as capital for the purposes of entitlement to income-based Jobseeker's Allowance or Income Support. See chapter 14 for information about benefits for people seeking work. If you receive contractual redundancy pay over and above the statutory minimum, this will affect when you will become entitled to claim Jobseeker's Allowance, as the amount in excess of the statutory minimum will be treated as earnings. You will therefore not be able to claim Jobseeker's Allowance immediately. When you will become entitled to claim depends on how much contractual redundancy pay you have been paid.

Contractual redundancy payments are not taxed, up to a sum of £30,000. So if your contract provides for a redundancy payment which is considerably more generous than the statutory minimum, or you negotiate this with your employer, you will have to pay tax on any part of the payment over £30,000.

Fixed-term contracts and redundancy

People are often surprised to find out that you can be entitled to a redundancy payment even at the end of a fixed-term contract. The contract has to have lasted at least two years for you to qualify for a payment. If the reason that the contract is not renewed is because the job is redundant, you will be entitled to a redundancy payment on the same terms as a permanent employee would be, even though it may always have been the case that the job was only expected to last for the fixed period. Note that, under the Fixed Term Employees (Prevention of Less Favourable Treatment) Regulations 2002, if you have been on a series of fixed-term contracts, which has lasted for more than four years, you will automatically become a permanent employee, unless your employer can justify keeping you on a fixed-term contract.

Redundancy over age 65

If you are aged over 65, or over your employer's normal retirement age if this is higher, your employer can retire you instead of making you redundant, even if your post will not be refilled. In this case you are not entitled to redundancy pay. But your employer will need to follow the retirement procedure, including giving you at least six months' notice and notifying you of your right to request not to retire.

Resolving Disputes

This chapter looks at ways of resolving disputes at work, either through informal methods or by using your employer's grievance procedure. It also looks at another option which involves reaching a formal settlement to resolve a dispute without starting a claim at an employment tribunal.

A dispute with your employer could arise in a number of ways: you may think your employer is denying you a right you have by law, for example they are not allowing you to take enough time off; or it could be a colleague who is creating a stressful environment for you to work in; or your employer could be trying to make changes to the way you work, for example by changing your hours or asking you to work in a different location. For information about your statutory and contractual rights at work, see chapter 2.

Of course, a dispute with your employer could also arise because of your own actions, in which case your employer should use their disciplinary and dismissal procedure to arrange a meeting to discuss this with you. Disciplinary and grievance procedures are designed to allow you and your employer to openly discuss problems and hopefully resolve them without recourse to the employment tribunal. See pages 52–53, for details of the statutory disciplinary and dismissal procedure.

In all of the situations described above it may be that you could take legal action by starting a claim at an employment tribunal or county court, but you should think carefully beforehand about whether there is some other way of resolving the dispute. Remember that formal legal action can take a long time before a final decision is reached, especially if one party decides to appeal a decision; it could be years before the case comes to an end. In addition, there's no guarantee that you will win your claim, no matter how strong you or your legal advisers think the case is. There may be something unexpected that comes out in the evidence, or some procedural or legal point which means that your claim fails.

You should also bear in mind that a tribunal claim can be very stressful, especially if it involves a dispute with people you used to work closely with. Your opponent may attempt to discredit you, or may criticise your performance, behaviour or attitude at work. If the claim reaches a hearing, you will have to give evidence and be cross-examined by your employer's representative. A final point to consider is that taking a tribunal claim all the way through to a final hearing can be extremely expensive if you have to pay for legal advice and representation. Funding issues at the tribunal are discussed in chapter 5.

So, although you may have the legal right to bring a claim at an employment tribunal, this should be seen as a last resort, only to be entered into if there is no other way of resolving the dispute.

ATTEMPTING TO REACH AN INFORMAL SOLUTION

The first step is usually to raise the issue informally with your employer. You would normally be expected to go to your own line manager, but if this is the person with whom you have the problem, you may well not feel comfortable doing so. Another manager should be prepared to listen in these circumstances. The situation may be different in a small company, where there could be only one person in a managerial position, compared with a large employer with a human resources department and many layers of management. In this situation, you might have to go straight to using the official grievance procedure, rather than trying an informal route first. It is for you to judge what is most appropriate, and what would be most effective.

If it is a colleague who is making things difficult for you, it may be a good idea to raise it with them first of all. With a case of potential harassment – in other words, when you're finding your colleague's behaviour intimidating or offensive – you should make it clear to them that you are not happy. It may be that they didn't realise their behaviour was upsetting you. If you think this is an overoptimistic scenario, and that approaching your colleague will just make things worse, raise the problem with a manager.

Unfortunately, the way a complaint is handled (by both parties) can sometimes lead to an escalation of the problem. You could even end up in a situation where you are more upset about the way your manager has dealt with the situation than by the problem you were complaining about in the first place. A lot depends on your employer's people-management skills and whether they have had effective training in handling disputes. And remember, your own approach to the problem also has a large part to play in whether the problem is resolved in a calm and reasonable way, or whether it descends into a full-blown dispute, perhaps ending in a tribunal.

If you are still in the early stages of a potential dispute with your employer, think about how you could best raise the issue with them. Try to avoid discussion with your manager or colleague at a time when you (or they) are angry or worked up about the issue; if you remain calm you will be more likely to be able to sort things out informally. Try to put yourself in your employer's position and, if possible, suggest practical alternative solutions to the problem. Give this some thought before you approach your manager.

If your grievance is about a problem which keeps recurring, rather than a one-off event, it could be helpful to keep a record of each incident. As well as helping you to remember details if the problem does end up in more formal action, this could be useful when discussing things with your employer to show that you haven't reacted hastily in raising the issue.

It's probably best not to threaten legal action immediately, but you should try to make sure you know what your rights are before raising the problem, and let your employer know that you have found out about the legal situation. This may be enough to get a result, without resorting to more confrontational action.

Perhaps most importantly, try not to leave it until things have got out of hand before addressing the problem.

TRADE UNIONS

If you are a member of a union, you should contact your union representative. They should have had training in how to support members during disputes and will probably have some experience of dealing with the management of your organisation. If the dispute cannot be resolved informally, the union may be able to provide you with legal advice and representation.

If you cannot resolve the matter with your line manager, you could approach a more senior manager, if you think this might help. Give your employer a reasonable time to sort things out, reminding them if necessary that you are still waiting for a resolution. But remember that there is a time limit (usually three months) for any tribunal claim you may want to bring, so don't leave it too long before taking more formal action if your employer is causing a delay. If this does not work, you should raise a grievance under your employer's official grievance procedure.

Although you're not required to write things down until you get to the official grievance procedure, it is a useful tool to keep your own written record of what has happened, and to write to people when face-to-face discussions haven't led to a resolution. Writing an email or memo provides a written record of your attempt to resolve a dispute, plus a chance to express yourself as clearly as possible.

GRIEVANCE PROCEDURE

Employers are required by law to have an official grievance procedure, as well as a disciplinary procedure, for employees to use if they want to make a complaint about anything related to work. Your employer should have given you details of their grievance and disciplinary and dismissal procedures within two months of you starting work for them, or within two months of October 2004 if you were already working for that employer when the new law came in. The law sets down minimum basic steps that must be included in your employer's grievance procedure.

The basic steps are:

1 You must put details of your grievance in writing and send it to your employer.

2 Your employer must then invite you for a meeting to discuss your grievance.

3 Your employer tells you their decision and must inform you that you have a right to an appeal meeting.

4 If you want to appeal, you should write to your employer explaining why you want to appeal. Your employer must then hold an appeal meeting and give you their final decision.

It may be that your employer has a more detailed grievance procedure which goes further than the basic steps. If so, you should make sure you follow that procedure.

Usually, you cannot start a tribunal claim unless you have raised a grievance in writing, and allowed your employer at least 28 days to respond to it. You are not expected to follow the grievance procedure if your complaint is about being dismissed, as you should appeal under the disciplinary and dismissal procedure instead. You *do* have to raise a grievance if you are claiming constructive dismissal (see p. 54), as the disciplinary and dismissal procedures do not apply to constructive dismissals. Also, if you have been dismissed but your complaint is about something other than the dismissal itself, for example you are owed unpaid wages or you were discriminated against, you still need to follow the grievance procedure. If you bring a tribunal claim without following the grievance procedure when you should have done, the tribunal could decide to decrease any compensation you are awarded by up to 50 per cent.

The time limit for bringing a tribunal claim is usually three months from the date of the incident you are complaining about, or from the last incident if it was a number of different events amounting to harassment. This time limit can sometimes be extended to allow you time to follow the grievance procedure. This will be the case in the following circumstances:

1 If you have submitted your grievance in writing to your employer, within the initial three-month time limit, you will automatically get an extension of another three months in which to submit your tribunal application. This is to allow you and your employer enough time to try to resolve the dispute between yourselves.

2 If you submit your tribunal application within the initial three months, without having first sent your grievance letter and

waited the minimum 28 days for your employer's response, your application will be returned to you. You will then be given an extension of a further three months, as long as you start your grievance within one month of the original three-month deadline.

For example, if you have a discrimination claim based on something that happened on 20 January, you have up to and including 19 April (three months) to submit your claim to the tribunal. If you do this within the time limit, but you have not first started the grievance procedure and waited 28 days, the application form will be returned to you. If you then start the grievance procedure by 19 May (one month from the original time limit), the time limit for submitting your tribunal application will be extended by three months (from the original deadline). So your new time limit will be 19 July. See chapter 5 for more details on tribunal time limits.

Disciplinary and dismissal procedure

There is a similar minimum procedure which employers must follow if they are considering disciplinary action against you, or if they are considering dismissing you. Under this procedure, your employer must set out in writing the reasons they are considering disciplinary action against you and, as with the grievance procedure, they must hold a meeting with you and give you the right to appeal. For information about dismissal from work, see chapter 3.

In any disciplinary or grievance meetings, you have the right to be accompanied, either by a trade union representative or by a colleague. If there is someone other than a union representative or a colleague who you particularly wish to attend the meeting, you can ask your employer but they have no obligation to agree to this.

MEDIATION

Mediation involves an independent third party who will work with the employer and employee to try to help them reach a mutually agreed solution to the dispute. Some employers (usually large organisations) have their own in-house mediation services, or might arrange for a specialist organisation to mediate in a dispute. If your employer does not offer this, you could suggest it to them as a way of resolving the problem without legal action, or you could contact an organisation such as the **Advisory, Conciliation and Arbitration Service** (ACAS) yourself.

ACAS is an independent, publicly funded organisation with a duty to attempt to help the parties in an employment dispute to reach a settlement. If you do start a claim at the tribunal, ACAS will automatically contact you about the possibility of resolving your dispute with their help. There is more information about ACAS's conciliation services in chapter 5.

You do not have to have started a claim to use ACAS's services. They may be able to mediate between you and your employer to try to reach an agreement, without the need for legal proceedings to be started. Because they are an independent organisation, they will not take sides in the dispute but will help both you and your employer to try to reach an agreement you are both happy with. ACAS can also provide information about your employment rights.

COMPROMISE AGREEMENTS

If your employer believes that there is a risk that you will bring legal action against them, they may try to end the dispute by offering you what is called a compromise agreement. This may either be because they believe you have a chance of winning a claim against them, or because they want to avoid the cost and trouble of defending any legal action, even if they think they will eventually win. A compromise agreement is a contract between you and your employer, under which you agree to give up your right to take legal action against your employer, in return for financial compensation.

The agreement will only be valid if you have had independent legal advice from a qualified person, and this person has signed the agreement. This is because in order to be able to judge whether your employer is offering you fair compensation for giving up your right to take future legal action, you have to be able to understand the nature and strength of any claims you may have, and what kind of compensation you may get if you were to successfully pursue those claims.

You should make sure that the advice you obtain includes advice on any potential effect that the agreement will have on your pension, particularly if the agreement involves your employment coming to an end earlier than it would otherwise have done.

Because the agreement will not be valid if you have not had legal advice, employers often offer to make a contribution to the cost of obtaining this advice. If your employer offers you this, you should ask them to confirm in writing that they will pay your adviser, even if as a result of their advice you decide not to sign the agreement. Otherwise you will have to pay for this yourself.

Employment Tribunals

If it has not been possible to resolve your dispute using an alternative approach, you might decide to start a claim at the employment tribunal (previously called the industrial tribunal). This chapter explains the procedure for doing so and suggests things to think about before deciding to go ahead.

You can obtain a list of the types of cases that employment tribunals deal with by calling the **Employment Tribunals** public enquiry line on 0845 795 9775. Or you could phone the **ACAS** helpline on 08457 47 47 47 to find out if the type of claim you want to make is covered

WHAT COULD YOU GAIN FROM A TRIBUNAL CLAIM?

Usually, assuming your claim is successful of course, the answer to this question is money. If your claim is for unfair dismissal, the tribunal can order your employer either to reinstate you into your old position, or to re-engage you in an alternative position within the organisation. This is often not practicable, as your employer may have appointed a replacement for you. Also the nature of the dispute may mean that there is no longer any trust between you and your employer and it may be impossible for you to go back to working together. The most common outcome is therefore a sum of money in compensation for the loss of your job. There is a section on the employment tribunal claim form (ET1) in which you can state if you wish to be reinstated or not. If you indicate that you do wish to be reinstated but your employer refuses to agree to this if you win the claim, you will be entitled to additional compensation.

COMPENSATION AT THE TRIBUNAL

Average awards of compensation at employment tribunals are lower than you might think from the stories you hear or read about, since the press tends to focus on only the highest awards. The following figures are the median awards for the different types of claim in the year 2005/06:

Unfair dismissal – £4,228

Race discrimination – £6,640

Sex discrimination – £5,546

Disability discrimination – £9,021

Compensation in a discrimination case is calculated by looking at what you have lost as a result of the discrimination. For example, if you have been dismissed you can claim for lost earnings, including future lost earnings up to the point where you are likely to find another job. Compensation can also take into account the loss of your employer's contributions towards your pension. You can also claim compensation for the emotional effects of the discrimination; this is known as an award for 'injury to feelings'. In some circumstances, where your employer has acted particularly badly, the tribunal may order them to pay an additional amount of compensation, to penalise them for their actions; this is known as 'aggravated damages'. For details of compensation for unfair dismissal see pages 54–55

Although the average payments are relatively low, there is no limit to the total amount of compensation that can be awarded in discrimination claims. With a claim for age discrimination, for example, the amount could be comparatively high, taking into consideration the fact that people over 50 are less likely to get back into work than younger people. There could therefore be high awards for the loss of future earnings. If your claim relates to unfair dismissal, rather than discrimination, the maximum amount that can be awarded in compensation is currently £67,100. For details of how compensation is awarded in unfair dismissal cases, see page 54.

You may well enter into the claim with the attitude that the compensation money is not the important thing for you and that what you really want is recognition that you have been treated badly and an apology from your employer. It is very unlikely that you will get an apology – the tribunal cannot order this – and even if the money really isn't important to you, you need to be realistic about how much you expect to be awarded if you win. If you are paying for advice and representation from a solicitor, and perhaps a barrister, there is a very real possibility that your legal costs will be more than the amount of compensation you are awarded. Ways of funding a claim will be looked at on page 81.

An important thing to remember is that very few cases lodged at employment tribunals make it all the way to a final hearing and judgment. ACAS figures for 2005/06 show that 76 per cent of applications made at tribunals were settled, withdrawn or dismissed before the final hearing.

Employers are often prepared to offer an amount of money to settle a claim, even if they think they will win, because it may work out less expensive than paying the legal costs of going all the way to a hearing.

If you agree to settle a claim, you will get compensation money but it is unlikely that your employer will admit any fault on their part, and the settlement will probably be on the grounds that it is kept confidential. So if you are looking for a public admission of guilt and an apology from your employer, this is probably not a good reason for starting a tribunal claim.

TIME LIMITS

There's a lot to do before deciding to make a claim: trying to resolve the matter informally; going through your employer's grievance procedure; getting legal advice and information. At the same time, it's vital you remember that there is a time limit for your claim. If you don't get your claim form to the tribunal within the time limit, it is extremely unlikely that you will be allowed to pursue your claim.

The time limit is usually three months from the date of the incident you are complaining of. So if you are only claiming unfair dismissal, for instance, the time limit will be three months from the date of the dismissal (this means the date your employment actually ends, not the date you were given notice).

If you are claiming discrimination, it can be more complicated, as the time limit, which again is three months, starts from the date when the discrimination occurred. This can sometimes be difficult to pinpoint. Say, for example, you have been refused a job on the basis of your age: the time limit would start running from the date of the decision not to invite you for interview or offer you employment, but there is unlikely to be any evidence of this; you may not have received any response at all to your job application. In this case the time limit would run from the date that other applicants were informed that they had been successful, but again you will probably not know when this was. There's no way around this uncertainty except to be particularly careful not to leave your application too late.

If you are claiming harassment, the time limit will start running from the date the harassment occurred; if it was a series of connected incidents that amounted to harassment, it would run from the date of the last incident.

Some types of claim have different time limits, although the majority are three months; for example, a claim for a statutory redundancy payment has a time limit of six months. To check the time limit for your particular claim, you should seek advice. See page 78 for a list of sources of free advice. In some circumstances the time limit can be extended in order to give you time to complete your employer's grievance procedure. See page 67 for details of when this will apply. You should seek legal advice before relying on getting such an extension to your time limit.

The most important thing is not to leave it until the last minute before putting in your application to the tribunal. If you have made a mistake in calculating the time limit, even if it is just one day, you will probably find that the tribunal will refuse to consider your application. They do have discretion to consider late claims, but you should *never* rely on this.

How to start a tribunal claim

The first thing to do when you have decided you want to go to a tribunal is to get some legal advice. It may be that, even if you feel you have been treated extremely unfairly by your employer, in legal terms you do not have a strong case. This could be because there is a lack of evidence, or it could be that, while your employer may have behaved badly, they may not have actually done anything unlawful. For example, if you have been forced to retire when you are over 65 and over your employer's normal retirement age, although you may feel this is unfair, it will not be unlawful if the employer has followed the correct procedure.

Independent advice

There are a number of sources of free, independent advice. Some of them provide basic advice on your legal rights; others may also be able to continue to provide casework and representation all the way to the conclusion of the case.

OPTIONS FOR OBTAINING FREE INITIAL LEGAL ADVICE

- Trade union – if you are a member of a trade union at the time the dispute arises, you should contact your representative for advice and assistance.

- **Citizens Advice** – see www.citizensadvice.org.uk or your local phone book for details of your local bureau.

- **ACAS** (the Advisory, Conciliation and Arbitration Service) see www.acas.org.uk – can answer questions on employment rights as well as offering a mediation service. Their helpline is 08457 47 47 47.

- *Law Centres* – these provide a free and independent professional legal service. See www.lawcentres.org.uk or your local phone book to see if there is a Law Centre in your area.

- Solicitors – some solicitors offer a free initial consultation. You should ask about how any further work they do for you could be funded. See the Law Society's website – www.lawsociety.org.uk – or your local phone book to find details of local solicitors specialising in employment law.

- **Age Concern** – some local Age Concerns can give information and advice on employment issues. See www.ageconcern.org.uk or call 0800 009966 for details of your local Age Concern.

- **Community Legal Service Direct** – see www.clsdirect.org.uk/index.jsp. This organisation runs a helpline for people who qualify for legal aid on 0845 34 5 4345 (England and Wales only).

- Law students – some universities and colleges which run law degrees or professional legal qualifications have programmes where law students give advice and possibly representation, under the supervision of their tutors. Contact your local university or college to find out if they run such a programme.

- Employee assistance schemes – some employers offer a confidential, independent helpline offering legal advice on matters which may include employment rights.

In addition to these organisations, as of October 2007, you will also be able to contact the **Commission for Equality and Human Rights** (CEHR) as a source of information and general advice. Part of the role of the CEHR will be to provide advice and support to people who are facing discrimination, including discrimination on the grounds of age. It will not have the resources to provide detailed legal advice or representation. For more information on the CEHR, see chapter 1.

How to arrange representation

If it looks as if you have a strong claim and you decide you want to go ahead, you then need to find out if you can get someone to help you prepare your case and to represent you at any hearings.

The difficulty here may well be the cost of getting legal representation. Unfortunately, legal aid funding for employment tribunal work is very limited: you cannot get legal aid funding for representation at the tribunal, only for a limited amount of preparation work. It is often very difficult to find a solicitor who will take on any legal aid employment work.

The other difficulty is that the rules on costs at employment tribunals mean that each party generally pays their own costs, regardless of the outcome of the case. This is different from the county court where the loser usually pays the winner's costs. This means that even if you have a very strong case and win your claim, you will still have to pay all your own legal costs if you have used a legal representative, such as a solicitor or barrister, who is charging you for their work. You may be able to get free advice and representation from an advice centre or Law Centre, or you may find that you have already paid for advice and representation, either through membership of a trade union, or through insurance.

OPTIONS FOR OBTAINING REPRESENTATION

- Citizens Advice – can sometimes provide representation, although resources at most bureaux are very stretched. All advice and representation will be free. See 'Options for obtaining free initial legal advice' box above for details.

- Law centres – again, these can provide free advice and representation but may have limited resources. See 'Options for obtaining free initial legal advice' box above for details.

- Trade unions – if you are a member at the time the dispute arises, trade unions can either provide representation themselves, or may refer your case to a solicitor. The union will usually be responsible for paying for the legal costs.

- Law students – contact your local university or college to find out if they run a programme for supervised law students to provide tribunal representation.

- Solicitor – you cannot get legal aid for representation at the tribunal but see below on options for how to fund solicitors' costs.

- Represent yourself – you do not have to have a representative. You can prepare and present your case yourself. This will be a challenge, but you may be able to obtain support or advice from one of the organisations above, even though they may not be able to represent you at the hearing.

- Anyone can represent you – they do not have to be legally qualified. You may have a friend or relative who has some relevant experience or knowledge who may be able to represent you effectively. There will be some changes to the rules on who can represent you, when a new system of regulation is introduced; this is expected to be in place in spring 2007. This will not affect individuals who help you voluntarily, so it will still be possible to have a friend or relative representing you on an unpaid basis.

How to fund solicitors' costs

If you pay for your own solicitor, unless you come to an alternative arrangement with them (see below), their fee will be calculated on the number of hours' work done on your case. This can be very expensive and difficult to predict and, as we've already seen, there is a risk that you could end up paying your solicitor more than you receive in compensation, with no guarantee of winning any compensation at all. You will be responsible for paying your solicitor's costs whether or not your claim is successful.

However, some solicitors will work on a 'no win no fee' basis (known as a contingency fee agreement). This is an agreement between you and your solicitor under which they agree to act for you on the basis that if your claim is successful, either through a settlement or if the tribunal finds in your favour, you will pay them out of your compensation. The agreement would usually be for you to pay a percentage of your compensation, generally somewhere between 25 and 50 per cent. If your claim is not successful, you will not have to pay your solicitor's costs although you will have to reimburse them for any expenses incurred while working on your case, such as the cost of obtaining an expert's report.

Another option is to check any insurance policies you have – in particular, household insurance – to see if legal expense insurance is included in your cover. If it is, check that employment tribunal claims are covered under this, and make sure that you comply with the requirements of the policy. For example, it is often a requirement that you notify your insurer of a dispute as early as possible. Your insurer may try to insist on your using a particular solicitor they have selected themselves, rather than a solicitor of your own choice. If you are not happy with this, you have the right to insist on using your own choice of solicitor, although insurers are often reluctant to agree to this and you may have to put up a fight. Your own solicitor should be able to help with persuading the insurers to allow them to act under the policy.

Depending on the terms of the policy, the insurance should cover your legal costs and expenses, but it is likely that the insurer will only agree to provide cover if you can show that you have a good chance of succeeding.

QUESTIONNAIRE PROCEDURE

If the claim you are considering relates to discrimination, you can request information from your employer, or whoever your claim is against, in the form of a questionnaire. Their answers should help you decide whether your case is worth pursuing, and allow you to gather evidence you would not otherwise have access to. We will look at the questionnaire procedure in the context of an age discrimination claim, but the same procedure is available for discrimination claims on the grounds of sex, race, disability, sexual orientation, religion or belief.

With discrimination claims it is often difficult to get evidence to support your case. You may believe that you have been discriminated against but have no conclusive evidence to prove it, as it's unlikely that there will be written evidence of discriminatory policies or practices, or an admission of discrimination from the employer.

While an employer is unlikely to admit on a questionnaire that they have acted unfairly, and some may ignore the questionnaire altogether, it does have a very useful function in that an employer may have had a valid reason for their actions which they can explain to your satisfaction. This is particularly useful if you have been unsuccessful with a job application and suspect that this was because of your age.

The questionnaire should be sent to the employer at an early stage: either before you submit your claim to the tribunal or, if you have already submitted it, within 21 days of doing so. There are standard questionnaire forms (for you) and response forms (for your employer) set out in the various pieces of legislation on discrimination. You do not have to use these forms; you could ask your questions in the form of a letter, or make adjustments to the standard form if necessary, but they are helpful to make sure you are asking appropriate questions. The questionnaire relating to age discrimination, produced by the Department of Trade and Industry, is reproduced from page 246. When you are drafting your questionnaire, you should set out the factual details of your complaint, explaining why you think the employer's treatment of you was unlawful. You then ask the employer to confirm whether they agree with your description of the facts and whether they agree that their treatment of you was unlawful. If they deny discrimination, you ask them to explain their reasons for their treatment of you and whether considerations of age (or whatever type of discrimination you are claiming) played a part at all.

You can also ask specific questions, as long as they are relevant and it is reasonable to expect the employer to answer them. If, for example, you think you have been refused a job because of your age, you could ask for statistical information such as the ages of all the applicants for the position, the ages of those shortlisted for interview and the age of the person who was ultimately successful. You can also ask for a breakdown of the ages of the existing workforce. If you found that people from a wide age range applied for the job but only people under 30 were shortlisted and there is no one aged over 40 working for the organisation, then the statistics would suggest a policy of not hiring people over a certain age. If you could show that you were qualified for the position, you would probably have done enough to show that discrimination *could* have taken place. It would then be for the employer to show that, in fact, age was not a factor in the decision and there was another fair reason for not recruiting you. However, if the statistics reveal that the person who got the job was actually older than you, you would probably decide against starting a claim.

You cannot force the employer to respond to the questionnaire, but the standard form explains that they have eight weeks to reply. If they fail to reply, or they do not answer all reasonable questions, or they give evasive answers, you can use the failure as evidence at the tribunal. You could suggest to the tribunal that the employer's failure to answer questions was a sign of having something to hide; a tribunal is entitled to draw an inference that discrimination has taken place, even if there is no concrete evidence of this.

BRINGING A CLAIM

To begin a claim at the employment tribunal, you need to complete form ET1 and return it to your local tribunal office. Remember the tribunal office must have received your form before the expiry of the relevant time limit (usually three months). See pages 68–69 for details of when the time limit can be extended to allow you to follow your employer's grievance procedure.

To obtain an ET1 form, phone the employment tribunals public enquiry line on 0845 795 9775 and ask them to send you one, or you can complete it online (www.employmenttribunals.gov. uk/claim_form_et1.asp). .

If you don't have an adviser to help you complete the form, you can still do it yourself. It is important to provide as much relevant detail as you can when explaining the facts surrounding your claim. You should include everything that you will want to rely on as part of your claim, so your opponent should not be taken by surprise by anything that you raise at the hearing. So, for example, if it is a claim for harassment on the grounds of age, you should include details of all the incidents you think amount to harassment, such as who said or did what and when.

You should state in detail what kind of claim you are making, so in an age discrimination case you should state whether you believe your employer's behaviour amounts to direct discrimination, indirect discrimination, harassment, victimisation or a combination of some of them. If you are also claiming unfair dismissal, or any other claim, this must be made clear. You should also explain why you think your employer's treatment of you was unlawful that is, why you think it counted as discrimination, unfair dismissal, unpaid holiday pay, or whatever claim you are making.

You can return your form by post, by delivering it in person, by fax or by submitting it online. If there is any doubt about the time limit, or you are within a few days of its expiry, it is obviously not a good idea to rely on the post.

The tribunal staff will send a copy of your claim form to your employer, so you do not need to do this yourself. Your employer will then have 28 days from the date the copy was sent to them in which to reply, by completing a response form (form ET3). Your employer can request an extension of the time limit, as long as they make the request to the tribunal before the 28 days are up. In the response form, your employer will have to state whether they intend to contest your claim, and if so, on what grounds. You will be sent a copy of the response form when this is returned to the tribunal.

THE ACAS CONCILIATION SERVICE

ACAS (the Advisory, Conciliation and Arbitration Service) is often in the news in connection with major industrial disputes between employers and unions, but actually most of its work involves sorting out problems between individual employees and their employers. ACAS is an independent, publicly funded organisation which has a statutory duty to attempt to promote settlement of employment disputes without the need for a decision by the tribunal. Conciliation is very similar to mediation, which was discussed on page 00; one difference is that a mediator may be more proactive in suggesting a solution, whereas a conciliator will support the parties in finding their own solution.

When the tribunal staff receive your claim form, they will pass your details to ACAS, who will contact you to discuss the possibility of reaching a legally binding settlement of the claim through conciliation. ACAS will also contact your employer. If you have a solicitor, or another representative, ACAS will deal with them rather than contacting you directly. It is therefore extremely important that you discuss the possibility of settling the claim with your representative, and make sure that they are clear about what you would want from any settlement. If your solicitor agrees a settlement on your behalf, you will be bound by it.

Conciliation works by having an independent person (an ACAS officer) trying to help you and your employer to resolve your dispute, without having to have the matter decided at a tribunal hearing. The ACAS officer will not give legal advice on your case, but talking things through with them can help you to see the strengths and weaknesses in your case and to identify what you would be happy with as an outcome. The ACAS officer works as an intermediary between you and your employer, putting forward offers from either party in an attempt to reach a settlement. This is usually done over the telephone, but conciliation could involve face-to-face meetings between the parties. Any settlement made as a result of ACAS's conciliation service is usually reached on the condition that it remains confidential, and the employer is likely to insist on this. However, this can be up for negotiation.

In many types of claim there is a fixed period during which conciliation with support from ACAS will take place. For unfair dismissal claims, this is 13 weeks from the beginning of the claim. For breach of contract, redundancy or unlawful deduction from wages claims, it is a shorter period of seven weeks. There is no fixed period relating to discrimination claims and so ACAS can continue to assist with conciliation right up until the date of the hearing, if this is appropriate.

Why go for a settlement?

There are many significant benefits to trying conciliation, rather than waiting for the tribunal to decide your case at a hearing. First, it is a way of getting the matter dealt with more quickly. Conciliation can begin immediately, whereas even with the simplest case you could be waiting months before you get a hearing and a decision. If you are paying a solicitor on an hourly basis, rather than under a contingency fee agreement, it will cost you much less if the matter can be settled quickly.

Then there is the inevitable stress involved with going to the tribunal. In particular, giving evidence and being cross-examined at the actual hearing are experiences that most people would rather avoid. If ACAS can help you reach a negotiated settlement with which you are happy, this would avoid the need to attend a hearing.

A significant benefit to conciliation, compared with a tribunal hearing, is that the settlement can be reached on any terms that the parties agree (as long as the agreement itself is legal). This means that the case does not have to be settled on the basis of monetary compensation alone, which is usually the only option available to a tribunal; for example you could negotiate for the settlement to include a requirement for the employer to give you a favourable reference.

Obviously, reaching a settlement through ACAS will involve some degree of compromise on both sides. You may have an idea of the maximum compensation you are likely to be awarded if your case succeeds at the tribunal. It is unlikely that your employer will offer you the figure you have in mind, unless they, or you, have been receiving poor legal advice. Of course, you are under no obligation to accept a settlement you do not agree with; if you wish to take your chances at the tribunal in the hope of receiving a larger settlement, that is up to you. Do keep in mind that, no matter how confident you or your adviser are in the strength of your case, there is never any certainty when it comes to the outcome of legal action. If you have a legal adviser who tells you that you will definitely win, you should consider seeking more realistic advice elsewhere.

When it comes to age discrimination, the law is so new that it could be particularly difficult to decide whether to settle a claim or go to the tribunal. It will be difficult to predict how the tribunals will decide cases under this new area of law and there will be very little previous case law with which you can compare your own case. This makes it all the more essential that you obtain good legal advice on any potential settlement, if you can.

Aside from the risk in each case that the tribunal could find against you at a hearing, there is also the possibility that you could win but be awarded significantly less than you had expected. It is hard to assess accurately the amount of damages likely to be awarded, unless it is a claim for a fixed amount of money, for example a claim for unpaid wages, or unpaid holiday pay. For discrimination claims it is particularly difficult.

These are all very good reasons for you to think seriously about any offer to settle the claim. Yes, you might get more if you went through with the entire process and yes, it can be hard to settle for less than you feel is your right; but if you can live with the settlement that has been offered, it could well be the best result for you.

Having said all that, you should only agree to a settlement if you want to. If you are confident in the strength of your claim, and that strength is based on good legal advice, then don't let yourself be bullied into settling the claim at an amount significantly less than it is worth. Your employer, or their representative, may try to persuade you to withdraw your claim by saying that they will apply to the tribunal for an order that you should pay their costs. In fact, the tribunal will rarely order you to pay costs (see p. 92 for details). Once you have agreed the settlement, it is legally binding and there is no going back. You will have signed away your rights to pursue the claim further so you must be happy with the settlement.

THE TRIBUNAL

There are 25 employment tribunal offices around England, Scotland and Wales, where cases are dealt with and hearings take place; to find your local office you can search on the website www.employmenttribunals.gov.uk, or phone 0845 795 9775.

The tribunal is usually made up of a panel of three people. The chairman (who of course could be a man or a woman) must be either a barrister or a solicitor who has been legally qualified for at least seven years. One of the other two members of the tribunal panel will be an employers' representative, probably with a background of having been an employer themselves; the other will be an employees' representative, probably from a trade union background. These two people will not be legally qualified.

The tribunal system was designed to be more informal than the court system (nobody wears wigs or gowns) but there are rules to be followed to make it as fair as possible for both parties. If you do not have a representative, the chairman is required to take steps to make sure that you are on an equal footing with your opponent. You may find that the chairman helps you out when it comes to following the correct procedures, but this will vary with different chairmen.

Soon after you submit your claim, the tribunal chairman will set out a timetable for you and your opponent to follow in preparing the case for a hearing. This will include stages such as preparing witness statements and exchanging them with the other side, and showing them any other evidence you will be relying on. It will also be decided whether any steps, such as ordering certain witnesses to give evidence, will be necessary. The chairman will estimate how long the final hearing will last. If it is expected to be for more than one or two days, and depending on how busy the tribunal is, it may be some months before there is enough free time in the diary for the hearing to be held.

If your case is quite complex you may have to attend a hearing to discuss the preparation of the case and agree a timetable. This hearing is called a *case management discussion* and can either be held at the tribunal office, or via a telephone conference.

Some cases may require an additional hearing called a *pre-hearing review*, to decide whether the claim should be allowed to continue, or to decide any outstanding issues to make sure everything is ready for the final hearing. However, most straightforward cases go directly to the *final hearing*. For the most simple case, for example a claim for unlawful deduction of wages, in which all that is to be decided is whether the employer owes unpaid wages to the employee, the final hearing could last only half a day, and the decision could be given to the parties on the same day.

For a more complex case, such as a discrimination claim, or a case where there are many witnesses to be heard, the hearing could go on for a number of days, or even weeks. You will usually need to be available all day on each day of the hearing.

At the tribunal hearing

If your claim is for discrimination, usually the claimant (you) gives their evidence first. If the claim is for unfair dismissal, it is usually the other way around, so the respondent (your employer) goes first.

You will be asked to give evidence; usually this is done by reading out a written witness statement you should have prepared beforehand. Once you have done this, the respondent, or their representative, will ask you questions – this is called cross-examination. Your representative, if you have one, will then be able to ask you questions in response to anything that has come up in cross-examination. After this, the tribunal members may have some questions to ask you.

If you have any witnesses, they will then give their evidence and be cross-examined in the same way.

Your employer and their witnesses will then give evidence (assuming you have gone first).

When all the evidence has been heard, the tribunal members will leave the room to consider their decision. If there is time, they will come back and give their judgement on the same day. In other cases, judgement could be reserved, which means you will be given the decision on a later date, usually by being sent it in writing.

If you have won your claim, the tribunal will decide how much compensation you should be awarded. It is possible that this could be done at a separate *remedies* hearing, at a later date, where you will give evidence on what losses you have sustained and, for a discrimination claim, how you have been affected emotionally. After this hearing, the tribunal will decide how much compensation to award.

If you are awarded a sum of compensation by the tribunal, your employer will be given a certain length of time by which they have to pay you. Unfortunately, if they do not pay, the tribunal itself has no powers to force them to do so. This means that you would have to start a separate claim in the county court (or sheriff court in Scotland) to get the tribunal's order enforced. Research by Citizens Advice estimated that one in twenty tribunal awards goes unpaid, requiring court action to be taken to enforce the tribunal's order. To find out about starting a county court claim, you should seek legal advice (see p. 78).

Although the general rule is that each side pays their own legal costs regardless of the outcome, in rare circumstances the tribunal can order you to pay your opponent's legal costs. This can only be done if the tribunal concludes that you have acted 'vexatiously, abusively, disruptively or otherwise unreasonably', or if your claim was 'misconceived'. So as long as you behave reasonably when bringing and conducting your claim, and your claim was not so weak that it should never have been brought in the first place, there should be no risk of having a costs order made against you.

Equally, if your employer is judged to have behaved 'vexatiously, abusively, disruptively or otherwise unreasonably', they could be ordered to pay your costs, if you are legally represented, or an amount to reflect your preparation time if you are not represented.

In practice, it is very rare for a tribunal to order one party to pay the other's costs. Even when such an order is made, it is usually for a relatively low amount, rather than an amount reflecting the party's actual costs. Although the maximum amount that the tribunal can order a party to pay is £10,000, the median costs order made in 2005/06 was £1,136.

Looking for Work

This chapter looks at how to find the right jobs to apply for, how to make an effective application and how to prepare for an interview. It also looks at how to deal with age discrimination as a potential barrier to finding a job.

If you have been made redundant after working for the same employer for a long time, it could be years since you have had to look for a job or attend an interview. Similarly, if you are looking to enter work for the first time after a long break – perhaps because you've had caring responsibilities up until now – you may find the idea of looking for work a bit daunting. But there are plenty of sources of help and support.

The starting point is to consider what type of work you are looking for. Don't necessarily discount the possibility of working for yourself – see chapter 9 on self-employment. If you have worked previously, think about whether you automatically want to look for the same type of work, or whether you want to broaden your options. Consider your experience, skills, and interests outside of any work you have done before, and whether these suggest a job which you might enjoy.

If you don't feel very inspired, don't worry; you may find that as you begin to look at job advertisements you get more of an idea of what you actually want.

When looking for jobs, be realistic about where you would be prepared to work. If you see an advert for what you think might be your dream job, but it's outside the geographical area you were looking in, you will have to think carefully about whether you really want to commute, or whether it would be practical to move home.

You also need to be realistic about the salary level of jobs you are searching for. If you are looking to change jobs or find a job quickly, you may have to broaden your search; this could mean looking at jobs that pay less than you currently earn, or would ideally like to earn.

KNOWING WHERE TO LOOK

There are thousands of different job vacancies advertised at any one time, so how do you make sure you get to find out about the right jobs for you? The more you look, the more likely you will be to find something suitable, so try a number of different approaches to job hunting.

If you are only looking for work that is local to you then it's probably best to start by looking at local sources of information, like a regional paper or a website with a local focus. If you only use national newspapers or job websites you could end up trawling through hundreds of inappropriate job descriptions before you find something relevant.

The internet

Many employers advertise vacancies on their own website. If there is a particular company or organisation you'd like to work for, you can visit their website and there is likely to be a section on current job vacancies, with information about the positions and how to apply.

Many jobs are also advertised on specialist job search sites on the internet. These sites allow you to search in a number of different ways, such as by location, field of work, or salary level. If you don't have the internet at home, you can use a computer at most local libraries, usually for free (although you may have to book a slot in advance). Alternatively, you could use an internet cafe, where you can pay anything between 50p and £2 per hour for use of the equipment.

SOME JOB SEARCH WEBSITES:

- National newspapers, such as www.guardian.co.uk; www.timesonline.co.uk

- Local newspapers. Many local papers also have a website. These are often called 'This is' and then the relevant geographical area, for example www.thisislondon.co.uk; www.thisisyork.co.uk; www.thisisgloucestershire.co.uk. These sites allow you to search for jobs in your local area.

- Specialist job search sites, such as www.jobsite.co.uk; www.jobsearch.co.uk; www.fish4jobs.co.uk; www.monster.co.uk

- Websites for jobs in particular sectors, for example www.jobsincharities.co.uk for jobs in the voluntary sector; or www.jobsinretail.co.uk for retail jobs.

- Jobcentre Plus Jobsearch website: www.jobcentreplus.gov.uk

Jobcentre Plus

Jobcentre Plus is the government agency responsible for helping people get back into work. It offers the largest national source of information about job vacancies. You don't have to be in receipt of social security benefits to use the Jobcentre Plus job search facilities although if you are on benefits, your personal adviser will be able to give you extra help with finding suitable jobs.

For information about other support you can get from Jobcentre Plus if you are on benefits see chapter 7.

There are a number of ways of looking for a job through Jobcentre Plus. You don't actually have to go to your local Jobcentre Plus to find out about the jobs listed on their database; this can be done over the phone or the internet, but if you want extra help, you can go along to your local office. The telephone service, called **Jobseeker Direct**, can give you details of suitable job vacancies. You can either access the service by phoning 0845 606 0234, which will be charged at a local rate, or you can go to your local Jobcentre Plus where there are telephones you can use, usually at individually partitioned desks to give you some privacy, which will connect you automatically to Jobseeker Direct for free. You then tell the helpline staff what kind of work you are looking for, and where, and they will give you details of any suitable jobs on their database. If there is a job that you are interested in, they can tell you how to apply and send you an application form. They may even be able to phone the employer and arrange an interview for you.

Alternatively, you can access the database of jobs advertised through Jobcentre Plus by looking on the website www. jobcentreplus.gov.uk. You start a job search on the website by selecting the area of work you are interested in, for example childcare/health/care, construction, managers or admin/office. You then choose a geographical area where you want the job to be based. If you only want to work at particular times, such as evenings, you can specify this as well.

The search will then give you a list of jobs which match your requirements and some details about the job. It will also give details of how to apply; this could either be applying directly to the employer, or you may have to call the Jobseeker Direct line with a reference number for further details on how to apply.

If you do not have access to the internet, you can do the same type of search by going to the Jobcentre Plus and using a Jobpoint. This is a touch-screen computer terminal, which will give you a list of suitable jobs which you can print off if necessary. You can then either use the free phones at the Jobcentre Plus to phone Jobseeker Direct to get details of how to apply for the jobs, or you can phone Jobseeker Direct from home.

Employment agencies

Another way of getting into work is to use an employment agency. Agencies are free to use for the person looking for work – fees are paid by the organisations who use them to fill vacancies. If an agency asks you to pay a fee for its services you should refuse to pay and you should report them to the **Employment Agency Standards Inspectorate**, a body run by the Department of Trade and Industry (DTI) which monitors employment agencies and handles complaints against them. The Employment Agency Standards Inspectorate runs an enquiry line on 0845 955 5105 which you can use if you want information about the rules agencies should follow.

Employment agencies can find you work on a permanent basis, in which case they're effectively introducing you to organisations who are looking to take on permanent staff; or they may find a fixed-term placement for you, perhaps for maternity cover, or a three-month contract. They often give you support and advice to help you through the preparation and interview process with a prospective employer; however, bear in mind that their priority is to find the right people for the employers who use them, and so if you don't match the criteria they may be less helpful than you would hope. It's usually a good idea to sign up with several agencies at once, and ring them on a regular basis to see if anything suitable has come up.

Alternatively, an agency can arrange a series of short-term placements with different organisations. This is known as 'temping', and in this situation your contract is with the agency, rather than with the organisations with which you are placed. Temping work can suit some people very well. It gives you the chance to broaden your experience and enhance your skills without committing to a long-term job in one place. It's flexible – you can turn down placements if you wish to – so can be ideal work to do while you're looking for something more permanent. You usually need to interview just once, with your agency, rather than each time you move to a new organisation.

As a general rule, most agencies will offer all of these services, so you may be provided with temporary work while the agency looks for a good permanent position for you. There is no limit to the number of agencies you can sign on with, so keep your options open.

The law on employment rights for agency workers can be unclear. Even if your contract with the agency states that no contract of employment will be created with the organisation with which you are placed, the circumstances under which you work may mean that, legally, you *are* an employee of that organisation. This will depend on things such as how much control the employer has over the way you work, whether you have an obligation to carry out the work and whether the employer has an obligation to provide you with the work. If you have a dispute with an employer with whom you have been placed by an agency, you should take legal advice on your status. See pages 19 to 21 for further details.

APPLYING FOR JOBS

Once you have found a job that you are interested in and have contacted the employer for further details, you will probably be sent an application pack, or the employer could request that you send a copy of your CV (curriculum vitae) along with a covering letter. An application pack should give you some extra information about the job and will help you to decide whether you really want to apply for it.

Application packs usually contain an application form as well as a job description and a person specification, which set out the skills, experience and qualities that the employer is looking for in the ideal candidate. Use the person specification to identify which skills and experiences you should emphasise when you complete the form, or when you prepare your CV. You should try to illustrate the skills you mention with evidence of how you have demonstrated them.

The application details may be available online, including an electronic version of the form for you to complete and return by email, rather than by filling out a paper version. Completing an electronic version can be easier than filling out a paper copy, as it is easier to amend what you have written and correct mistakes. Take extra care over grammar and spelling, especially if you are applying for a job that requires good written communication skills; if necessary, ask someone to read it through before you send it off.

You may be asked at the application stage to provide details of people who can give you a reference, although it is likely that your referees will not be approached until after the interview stage. You should think about who would be the most suitable people to give you a reference, and contact them in advance, if you can, to make sure they are happy to do so. It should be someone who has recent relevant contact with you, like your last employer, or if you have recently taken a course at college it could be your tutor. If you don't include your current or most recent employer as a referee, the recruiter will probably want to know why. If you have been involved with voluntary work, your referee could be someone who worked with you at the organisation. You should try to avoid using a friend unless there is another good reason why they are suitable, and you should never use a family member.

CVs

A CV is a summary of your qualifications, achievements, skills and work experience which should be laid out as neatly and concisely as possible. Ideally, it should be no more than two pages, although you may need to write a longer one for some posts. It is a way of giving a prospective employer important information about yourself to persuade them to employ you. You should make sure that the information on your CV is relevant to the particular job for which you are applying. This means that you should not always use a standard CV to send to all employers: you could cut some less relevant sections while expanding on those that will be of most interest to a prospective employer. For example, if you are using your CV to apply for a job which has a person specification, you should make sure that the details on your experience and qualifications meet the specific requirements of the job.

You do not have to include your age or date of birth on your CV. It will be for you to decide whether you want to or not. Similarly, if you have formal educational qualifications that you gained a long time ago, you don't have to include the date of the qualification.

Many employers will not require you to send in your CV but will ask you to complete their application form instead. In this case do not send in your CV as it will only irritate the recruiter. Your CV will be very important though if you are contacting employers on a speculative basis, asking them to consider you for work, rather than replying to an advert.

If you are over 50, you have obviously got more time to cover in your CV compared with a younger person. You may have taken formal qualifications a long time ago, which may not seem particularly relevant to the work for which you are now applying. If you've been out of work for a while, you might be worried about what to do about gaps in your work history. You should emphasise your experience, skills and qualifications which are most relevant to the job you are applying for, even if these were not gained in paid employment. For example, if you have never had a job that required you to use computers, you may nevertheless have gained computer skills outside of work and this should be included in your CV. If your work history is lengthy and takes up too much space in your CV, you can omit jobs which you held a long time ago, or which do not appear relevant to the job you are applying for. Alternatively, you could summarise jobs by grouping them together, rather than giving details on each position.

When considering what is relevant to the position, don't just think about the type of work involved. You should also concentrate on experience and skills you have gained, perhaps in a completely unrelated field of work, which could nevertheless be relevant, such as supervisory responsibilities, or skills related to contact with clients or managing difficult situations.

If you are claiming benefits, you may well be able to get help from the **Jobcentre Plus** with preparing your CV. Alternatively, if you sign up with an employment agency, staff there will also be able to help. There are also firms that provide help with writing CVs but these are very likely to charge for their services.

SUGGESTED ADVICE ON DRAFTING YOUR CV

- Use a computer or word processor. Make sure it looks professional. Don't use a typewriter as this may set off alarm bells as to your familiarity with IT, in even the most well-intentioned, non-age-discriminatory employer. Use a sensible, modern font, like Times New Roman, Arial, or Verdana. Always use the spell check.

- Two sides of A4 is generally the ideal length. Even if the information you include is relevant and interesting, it is unlikely that you will hold the attention of the employer for three sides. Remember, they're reading lots of other CVs too, and will appreciate a concise summary of your experience.

- If you have had many different jobs, you can leave out the ones you held a long time ago, or which are not relevant to the job for which you are applying.

- You do not have to include your date of birth. It is up to you to decide whether you want to.

- Use headings and section breaks. Don't try to squeeze too much information into the two sides of A4. Try to space the text out so that it is easy to read. Stick to a consistent format throughout.

- Start with your most recent job, or work-related experience, and work backwards.

- Use bullet points rather than long paragraphs.

- Don't include details about interests and activities outside of work, unless it is something relevant to the job, or illustrates a relevant skill or position of responsibility.

- Put in contact details, including an email address – if you don't have an email address, you can set up an account for free. However, remember that employers might use it to contact you and so if realistically you will not check it regularly, you should leave this out.

- Include details of what you achieved in a particular role, not just a description of what the role was.

- Back up skills that you claim to have with evidence. So for example, rather than simply saying you have good telephone skills, you could give an example of a role where you dealt effectively with customer complaints over the telephone.

- Don't use 'Curriculum Vitae' as a heading; your name should be at the top of the page.

INTERVIEWS

Don't expect that you will automatically get the first job that you are interviewed for. If you do not get the job, it doesn't necessarily mean that you were not suitable, or that you performed badly at the interview – it is probably just that there was someone else who applied for the job who the employer thought was better suited. Then again, if you really did do badly in the interview it's not the end of the world. Consider calling the organisation for some feedback – many employers are happy to provide this, and some actually offer it – and think over the mistakes you feel you've made and how to avoid them next time. Performing well at interviews is a skill in itself and so you could look at every interview you have as useful experience for the next one. You will probably find that it gets easier with practice.

It is essential to prepare well for an interview. This means making sure that you know about the organisation and what the particular role involves. If the organisation has a website, or publicity materials, make sure you look at these in detail, taking notes and preparing your own questions.

You should prepare for the types of questions you will be asked. Obviously, you will not be able to predict exactly what the questions will be, but there are likely to be some which you can expect. You should refer to the job description, and person specification if there is one, and prepare to speak about how you fit the requirements. You might be asked to refer to particular examples of times when you have done something like working in a team, or working to a deadline. Before the interview, think back over your past work experience, and also your experience outside of work, and try to identify some particular situations you might be able to talk about. Some popular questions that you should be prepared to be asked are:

What are your strengths and weaknesses?

What relevant experience do you have for this job?

Why have you applied for this job? (This one is very important as it will help you consider whether the job is really for you.)

What can you bring to this position?

Have you seen our website? What did you think about it? What's your impression of the organisation?

What positions of responsibility have you held? How did you deal with them?

Tell me about a time when you have had to deal with a difficult person.

Tell me about a time when you have worked as part of a team. What was your role?

Tell me about a time when you have had to work to a deadline or juggle different priorities.

Are there any areas of training or development you would like to pursue if you were successful in obtaining this job?

Why did you leave your last job?

How would other people describe you?

What is your greatest success? What are you most proud of?

You might find that it helps to rehearse answering these questions out loud, or at least spend some time thinking about how you would answer them. Many of the answers you come up with will help you to identify areas you could refer to in answers to other questions not listed here. You could ask a friend to look at the information you have about the job and then think up some questions for you to practise.

When answering, refer to past experience; it doesn't have to be work-related, but it should be relevant. Don't just say you're good at something; give an example of when you have done it and how you succeeded.

You will almost certainly be asked about specific things that you have mentioned in your CV or application form, so be prepared to talk about things you have done before, such as previous jobs, work experience or courses. Try to pick out skills and experience which will be particularly relevant to the job you are applying for and rehearse talking about these. It's fine to take a copy of your CV or application form to refer to in the interview.

At the end of the interview you will probably be asked if you have any questions for the interviewer. Try to think of some questions in advance. They could be about the organisation in general or about the particular job. For example, you could ask about the department you will be working in, and who you will be working with, or what kind of training could be available if you are successful. Don't ask too many questions, but enough to show you are interested in the organisation and the position.

In the interview, make sure that you listen to each question carefully, and answer it directly. Don't just talk about what you have prepared, or what you want to talk about, if it doesn't actually answer the specific question you have been asked. You should try to strike a balance between not saying enough and saying too much, or rambling. An ideal answer could be approximately one minute long, but this will obviously depend on the question.

Try to sound positive, confident and enthusiastic when answering questions. Be aware of your body language, so try not to fiddle with things in front of you such as a pen or papers.

You should dress smartly, but what you wear to the interview will depend on what kind of job you are applying for, so you don't want to look too showy, or dress in a way which will distract attention from what you are saying. A good rule to follow is to dress one notch smarter than the people who actually do the job.

You may feel nervous before you go into the interview. People cope with nerves in different ways, some well, some badly. The best cure for nerves is good preparation, but another helpful tip is to try and speak to someone just before you go into the interview. You might find that it helps to relax you a little if you call someone and have a quick two-minute conversation, or make small talk with the receptionist.

AGE DISCRIMINATION IN RECRUITMENT

You might be worried that you will be at a disadvantage when applying for jobs because of your age. There is no getting away from it – people over 50 (and even younger than this) can suffer from age discrimination when trying to get work.

Discrimination on the grounds of age is more prevalent in some sectors than others, and so depending on what kind of work you are looking for, this may not be an issue for you. But if you feel that it is a problem, it is useful to know your rights and how to deal with possible discrimination.

Up until October 2006, there was no protection against discrimination on grounds of age. Even now that we have the Employment Equality (Age) Regulations 2006, protection against age discrimination in recruitment is seriously limited when it comes to people over 65. An exemption included in the regulations means that employers can lawfully exclude from their selection procedure anyone over 65, or over the normal retirement age the employer has set, if this is higher. This means that employers can reject candidates solely on the grounds of their age, without the candidates having a chance to challenge this. Employers can rely on this exemption to reject any candidate who is within six months of their 65th birthday (or the birthday on which they reach the employer's normal retirement age, if this is higher) when they apply for the job.

It is to be hoped that the new law will highlight the issue of age discrimination in a way that will encourage employers to review their recruitment practices with regard to decisions based overtly, or subconsciously, on age. It is likely to take a long time for the necessary culture change to take place so that we reach a point where age is no longer a factor in recruitment decisions.

However, if you are more than six months away from your 65th birthday, you are protected by the new law. As is discussed in chapter 4, legal action may not always be the best way of resolving a dispute, but, particularly when it comes to possible discrimination in recruitment, there is sometimes no effective alternative. You have the option of bringing an age discrimination claim against a potential employer if you believe that the reason you didn't get the job was your age, or that some aspect of the recruitment procedure put you at a disadvantage because of your age.

To be successful, you would have to have evidence to show that age discrimination could have taken place. The type of evidence you would need would depend on the facts of your case but it could be that you were asked your date of birth on the application form; or the wording of the job advert suggested they were looking for a younger candidate; or there could have been a comment or question at the interview along the lines of 'Aren't you too senior for this role?'; or it could simply be that you were better qualified for the role than the person who got the job. None of these things would be conclusive proof of discrimination, but they could be evidence suggesting that discrimination could have taken place. It would then be for the employer to prove that there was another reason for their decision not to hire you, and that they had not discriminated against you.

It can be difficult to prove any type of discrimination when it comes to recruitment, as the employer is unlikely to admit they have acted unlawfully, and there may be little evidence to support your case. There is a procedure you can use under the age regulations whereby you can send the employer a questionnaire, requesting information such as the ages of the current workforce, the people who applied for the job, those who were selected for interview and those who were successful (see pp. 82–84). The standard questionnaire form is reproduced from page 246.

If you are successful in winning a tribunal claim, you will be awarded compensation for the loss of the opportunity to take the job. However, rather than having the chance to go to an employment tribunal and be awarded monetary compensation, what you would probably prefer is to be offered the job in the first place. The way to go about that is to prepare your CV or application form as well as possible to try to counteract any ageism on the part of the employer. If you are offered an interview, you can hopefully use your performance at the meeting to dispel any concerns the employer may have about your age.

Support When You're Out of Work

If you have recently found yourself out of work, you will probably already have spent time considering your options. Most people want to get back into work as quickly as possible. On the other hand, you might ask yourself whether you actually want to go back to work; perhaps you feel that your days in the workforce are over and the time has come to enjoy your retirement. For many people financial considerations mean that giving up work is not realistic. But even if you have a retirement income that you're happy with and money isn't an issue, you may not feel ready yet to give up work for good. Many people want to go on working for other reasons, such as enjoying the contact with friends and colleagues, and being able to continue using their skills to do something productive and useful. It's not so unusual to actually enjoy going to work. If you are in this position but are finding it difficult to get the job you want, you could consider volunteering, or self-employment (see chapters 9 and 10 for further information on this).

If you've just started looking for a job, don't worry if you don't find something immediately. While it's true that people over 50 can find themselves at a disadvantage when seeking work, don't assume this will inevitably happen to you and don't give up hope, even if you go for a long time without finding the work you want. The important thing is to make sure you have access to all the support available that could be suitable for you. This could be practical work-focused training, or advice and support in overcoming barriers to work and increasing your personal confidence. Much of the support available is aimed specifically at people who have been out of work for some time and at those who are currently claiming benefits.

This chapter looks at the support services available for people who are out of work but want to get back into employment. It focuses mainly on government-provided support programmes accessed through the **Jobcentre Plus**, but bear in mind that there are many services provided by the private sector that may be more suitable for you. There are a number of organisations such as recruitment agencies or career guidance counsellors who offer advice, access to training and help with applications, as well as matching you to suitable jobs. There are some agencies which specialise in helping older people to get into work. **The Age and Employment Network** can refer you to organisations which may be able to help.

You can also find helpful information in chapters 6 and 8 on looking for work and improving your skills.

Most of the government support is for people receiving welfare benefits, and there are specific programmes for people aged over 50 and people who are on benefits for health reasons. This chapter mentions financial support which is available as part of specific programmes, but for detailed information on social security benefits and additional financial support, see chapter 13.

JOBCENTRE PLUS SUPPORT

For many people, the starting point for access to support with getting into work will be **Jobcentre Plus**. This is the government agency formed from a merger of the former Employment

Service and parts of the Benefits Agency (it was expected that the rebranding of social security, benefits agency and Jobcentre offices to Jobcentre Plus would be completed by 2006, but in some areas Jobcentre Plus services may be provided at an office which is still called a Jobcentre or a social security office). It is responsible for both benefits and job-search services for people looking for work. It can help you by providing advice and support, including access to training, whether you wish to find a job or become self-employed. Jobcentre Plus deals with benefits for people who are out of work and under state pension age.

You will find that some of their services and schemes are only available to people who have already been claiming certain benefits for some time. If you are in this position, this chapter will give you information about what extra help you could be entitled to. If you have only just started claiming benefits, it may be worth asking at your Jobcentre Plus about these schemes, as they are sometimes made available to people at an early stage. For example, this may be the case if you have a disability or health problem. If you have not yet claimed benefits but want more information about what you might be entitled to you should ask at the Jobcentre Plus.

Basic support

The main benefit for people looking for work is Jobseeker's Allowance. It is available on condition that you are actively trying to find a job. When you begin a claim you will have an interview with an adviser during which you will discuss what you can do to improve your prospects of getting work. You and your adviser will agree the actions you will take to look for work and they will be written down in a Jobseeker's Agreement which you will both sign. Every two weeks you are required to attend follow-up meetings to discuss the steps you've been taking to find work. Over time Jobcentre Plus will usually expect you to look for a wider range of jobs, for example in a different occupation or further from your home, as this will improve your chances of finding work.

Anyone, whether or not they are claiming benefits, has access to some Jobcentre Plus services, including Jobpoints and the **Jobseeker Direct** telephone line. For information on these services, see chapter 6.

The New Deal

The New Deal programmes provide access to a range of support – for example hands-on help from a personal adviser, training or self-employment trials – aimed at meeting the needs of the particular individual. There are a number of different New Deal schemes including New Deal for Disabled People, New Deal for Partners, and New Deal for Lone Parents. The most relevant for this book is New Deal 50 Plus, which, as the name suggests, is for people aged 50 and over. New Deal 50 Plus is a voluntary programme, although the government is proposing to test compulsory participation in some parts of the country. Depending on where you live, if you are under 60 you may also have to take part in New Deal 25 Plus once you have been receiving benefit for 18 months. The New Deal programmes are accessed through your local Jobcentre Plus, except for New Deal for Disabled People which you can also sign up for through independent providers.

You usually have to have been out of work for at least six months before you can join a New Deal 50 Plus scheme. You must also have been receiving benefits (either Income Support, Jobseeker's Allowance, Incapacity Benefit, Severe Disablement Allowance or Pension Credit), or National Insurance credits, or have been the partner of someone who claims benefits. In special circumstances it may be possible to start earlier without having to wait six months, so always check with your Jobcentre Plus about whether you might be eligible.

If you join a New Deal scheme, you will be given advice and support to help you look for work, on a one-to-one basis from a New Deal personal adviser. You will have an initial interview with your adviser to discuss any work experience you have, your current situation and what type of work you would like to find. You will then draw up an action plan together which will identify ways of improving your chances of finding work. This could include undertaking training or voluntary work if these options would be appropriate for you. Your personal adviser will give you ongoing support with looking for jobs and applying for them.

You might consider self-employment as an alternative to looking for work with an employer. New Deal 50 Plus can provide you with access to advice and support with starting your own business. For more information on self-employment, see chapter 9.

If you start work after taking part in New Deal 50 Plus, you will also be eligible to claim an in-work training grant of up to £1,500. You can apply for this grant up to two years from when you start working. It can be used for training relevant to your new job, or up to £300 of it can be used for training or learning which may not be immediately relevant to your current job but which could help you realise your longer term career plans.

If you start work or become self-employed, having been in receipt of any of the benefits mentioned above for at least six months (whether or not you have taken part in the New Deal 50 Plus scheme), you could be eligible for the 50-plus element of Working Tax Credit to provide you with extra income on top of your earnings. This can be paid for up to 12 months after you start work, but you must apply for it within three months of starting your new job. See chapter 12 for more information on Working Tax Credit.

If you are on a New Deal scheme, you can get discounts on travel on rail services in England and Wales and discounts on London buses and London Underground. To obtain the discounts you will need to get a photocard from your Jobcentre Plus.

Work Trial and Employment on Trial

The Work Trial and Employment on Trial schemes give you the opportunity to try out a job, without your benefits being affected if it doesn't work out. This can give you the chance to prove you are suitable for the job and to find out if the job is right for you. A Work Trial is a short-term scheme lasting for up to 15 days. Employment on Trial can last up to 12 weeks, but you must stay in the job for at least four weeks or your entitlement to benefits may be affected.

Programme Centres

Support with finding work arranged through the Jobcentre Plus is sometimes provided by Programme Centres. The centres are run by local independent organisations under contract to Jobcentre Plus and so the services and courses available will vary depending on where you live. Programme centres are not available in all areas. If your area does not have a programme centre, you should still be able to access the same types of service through your Jobcentre Plus. You usually have to have been claiming a relevant benefit for at least six months but you should check with your Jobcentre Plus adviser whether you are eligible to use a programme centre. The purpose of Programme Centres is to help people develop skills needed to find and keep a job.

Information is provided, with individual support from a trained adviser on various modules such as:

• overcoming barriers to work (this could include how to deal with age discrimination);

• advice and support with job searching;

• preparing a CV;

• completing application forms;

- interview techniques.

The centres also have resources, such as computers with internet access and word-processing programmes, printers and photocopiers, which can be used for free.

Work Based Learning for Adults

Work Based Learning for Adults (WBLA) programmes (called Training for Work in Scotland) provide skills training, usually for people who have been out of work for at least six months, to improve their chances of finding a job. It can involve training in completely new skills, or updating existing skills in which you may not have had recent formal training. The training can lead to formal qualifications.

The programme can include training to prepare you for self-employment, such as advice and support on preparing a business plan, and then an opportunity to run your business on a test-trading basis. See chapter 9.

WBLA also provides training in basic skills such as reading, writing and maths, and can include English language skills if English is not your first language.

People who undertake WBLA training receive a training allowance of an extra £10 a week on top of their normal benefits.

The programme can sometimes be available to people who have not yet been out of work for six months and so it is worth asking about this, or any other skills training that may be available.

Help for people receiving health-related benefits

If you receive health-related benefits, the support available to you to help you get back into work will depend on where you live. There is a new scheme described below which operates in some areas of the country. If you are not covered by this new scheme, there will still be support available to you under existing government programmes.

No matter where you live, if you make a new claim for an incapacity-related benefit – Incapacity Benefit or Income Support (for health reasons) – you will have an initial interview with a specialist adviser eight weeks later to discuss your work options.

If you have a disability or health problem and want to get into work, there is additional support available at the Jobcentre Plus from specialist Personal Advisers or Disability Employment Advisers. They will help you assess what kind of work could be suitable for you and put you in touch with employers. Disability Employment Advisers can also help people already in work if they are concerned about losing their job for a reason related to their disability. If you are in this situation, you should be aware of your rights under the Disability Discrimination Act. See chapters 2 and 14 for more details on this.

You will have access to the other programmes described in this chapter, as long as you meet the relevant eligibility criteria, as well as those designed specifically to assist disabled people, such as the WorkPath programmes and the New Deal for Disabled People.

WorkPath programmes provide practical support and advice to help you overcome specific barriers to work related to your disability. If you have a Disability Employment Adviser at a **Jobcentre Plus**, they should discuss with you whether any of these programmes might be suitable for you. WorkPath may be available to you even if you are not claiming benefits, and even if you already have a job. Disability Employment Advisers can help people already in work, and their employers, if they are concerned about losing their job for a reason related to their disability. If you are in this situation, you should be aware of your protection under the Disability Discrimination Act. See chapter 14 for details on this.

New Deal for Disabled People is a similar programme to New Deal 50 Plus (described above), for people receiving disability or health-related benefits. Depending on where you live, it may be referred to by a different name. Under the New Deal for Disabled People you will work with a job broker, which will be a specialist company or disability charity working under contract to Jobcentre Plus. They will help to match your skills, experience and abilities to the needs of local employers. The scheme can include access to training if this is appropriate. Local providers sometimes recruit clients directly, for example through leaflets or by setting up on high street locations. If you sign up for a job broker directly, you will need to prove you are claiming health-related benefits.

New Deal for Disabled People is usually only available to people under state pension age (age 60 for women and 65 for men) although there may be exceptions to this rule in special circumstances.

The new system – Pathways to Work A new system of support for people on health-related benefits is being introduced gradually. Pathways to Work, sometimes known as Choices, operates as a pilot project, initially in around a third of the country. From 30 October 2006 it is extended to more areas of the country and will be operating nationwide by April 2008. You should ask your Jobcentre Plus adviser if the area you live in is covered.

Pathways to Work is aimed at people with a health problem who are claiming Incapacity Benefit, Income Support (for health reasons) or Severe Disablement Allowance. The programme offers access to many of the existing support services mentioned in this chapter, such as Work Based Learning for Adults and Work Trial, but also introduces new services – with involvement by the NHS – to help people manage health problems which may otherwise be a barrier to work.

Under the scheme, depending on your health condition and prospects of finding work, you may be required to attend a programme of interviews and your benefit can be reduced if you do not attend. The government stresses, however, that the programme is not intended to be a way of forcing people back into work when they are not ready. Rather, the aim is to provide practical and financial support, through more contact with Jobcentre Plus advisers at an early stage and through contact with healthcare professionals.

If you make a claim for Incapacity Benefit, or Income Support on health grounds, you will have an interview with a trained incapacity adviser at the Jobcentre Plus eight weeks after the start of your claim. The adviser will decide whether you could benefit from Pathways to Work and, if so, you will have to attend up to five more compulsory interviews over the next six months. This is a significant difference from the previous system for people on incapacity benefits, under which you would have been required to attend only one interview. If the adviser decides that your disability or health condition is such that you would not be expected to return to work in the foreseeable future, you will not have to attend further interviews, unless you choose to take part in the scheme voluntarily. Similarly, if the adviser thinks that you already have good prospects of returning to work without participating in the scheme, you will not be expected to take part.

If you are already claiming an incapacity-related benefit when the Pathways to Work pilot starts in your area, you can choose to take part, although it is compulsory for those making new claims.

At the work-focused interviews, the adviser will discuss with you what your aims are, in terms of what kind of work you would like to do and would be able to do. They will help to identify any potential barriers, health-related or otherwise, to finding suitable work, and will try to find ways of overcoming these barriers; this could include involvement of the NHS. An action plan of steps to be taken will be drawn up and reviewed over the series of interviews.

People taking part in Pathways to Work may be referred to a Condition Management Programme run locally by NHS providers. The idea is that these programmes will help you manage your condition, and so rather than providing treatment, they will provide access to services such as counselling, exercise programmes, and help with stress and pain management.

There is a financial incentive for people who start work after being on receipt of an incapacity benefit for at least 13 weeks. If you do start work again, you will be paid a Return to Work credit of £40 a week on top of your wages. The credit is tax free and will be paid for the first year after you return to work, as long as you work at least 16 hours a week and your annual salary is expected to be £15,000 or less. You can also claim the Return to Work credit if you become self-employed.

If you take part in Pathways to Work, you may also be eligible to receive support under New Deal 50 Plus at the same time. If this is not offered to you, you should ask your adviser, as this could lead to entitlement to the in-work training grant if you return to work.

Permitted work If you are not working because of ill-health or a disability and you are receiving an incapacity-related benefit, you are allowed to do a limited amount of work without it affecting your entitlement to your benefits.

Permitted work can allow you to try paid work, without worrying about losing your entitlement to benefits if it doesn't work out.

There are three circumstances in which work will count as 'permitted work':

1 If you earn less than £20 each week you work;

2 If you work for less than 16 hours a week and earn up to £81. This period of work should last for a maximum of 26 weeks, but can be extended by another 26 weeks if your Jobcentre Plus adviser or job broker agrees to this.

3 If you earn less than £81 a week doing work supervised by or on behalf of a public body or voluntary organisation, for example in a sheltered workshop. This option is for people who may not be able to work without considerable ongoing support, due to significant health problems or disabilities.

You must inform your benefits office in writing about the work you are doing either any time during the period you are doing it, or, in the case of option 2 above, within 42 days of starting.

Regional variations

Unfortunately, recent budget cuts have led to reductions in funding for some of the programmes mentioned above, in particular in resources for WBLA and the self-employment support it provides, and in the provision of specialist New Deal 50 Plus advisers. However, there are a number of different pilot projects being trialled around the country, and so, depending on where you live, there could be services available which are not mentioned above. In almost all cases, your first port of call should be your local Jobcentre Plus. They can tell you exactly what is available, and run through all the schemes and benefits you are entitled to take advantage of in your area.

There may also be local projects which are not provided through Jobcentre Plus, particularly in areas of high unemployment. These could be backed by local authorities, or with funding from the European Union. Again, your Jobcentre Plus should be able to advise you of what additional support is available.

Skills and Qualifications

This chapter looks at learning new skills as a route to finding work, changing your job or improving your prospects in your current career. Training courses will give you new skills and can also lead to recognised qualifications, which provide evidence of what you can do. Recent training should help you stand out from the crowd during the selection process for recruitment or promotion, as it will show employers that you are serious about the job. It can also help you work more effectively in your current role and can enhance your job satisfaction.

Many people also learn for personal pleasure or to achieve something outside work. For example, foreign languages and courses related to interests such as photography or art are very popular. However, this chapter only looks at learning that is linked to work. The education system for adults is different in England, Scotland, Wales and Northern Ireland. This chapter is about England only.

WORKING OUT YOUR OPTIONS – ADVICE AND GUIDANCE

You may know exactly what training you need to achieve the goal you have set yourself. For example, you may know that you will need to gain a professional qualification before you are eligible for promotion. Or if you decide to change career and become a teacher you will obviously need to enrol in teacher training. But often people don't have very clear career plans, or know exactly how new skills or qualifications might help. Working practices and expectations about skills could have changed significantly since you were last job-hunting; you may want to change your job but not know what else you could do; or you might be out of work and keen to identify jobs which fit your skills and interests, or where there is a local shortage so that you will have a good chance of finding a job.

In these and many other situations, training can open the door to new opportunities and a more satisfying working life. The first step is to decide where you want to be in the future, whether it's in the same job but with more confidence, or doing something completely new. Then you can go about acquiring the skills to make this happen.

Once you have decided what work you want to do, you still may not know exactly what experience, skills and training you will need. Happily, there are many sources of advice about careers and training. One of the first places to start is **learndirect**. This is a government agency which holds the details of the courses provided by every major training provider in the country, as well as providing its own computer centres and online courses. Their website and telephone advice line are an excellent source of information about skills and work. Visit the learndirect website on www.learndirect.co.uk, or call their free national telephone advice service on 0800 100 900.

If you want more support than it's possible for an adviser to give over the phone, you can get personalised help from **nextstep**, a national network of careers guidance agencies. Each agency offers free access to information materials and they also offer face-to-face guidance sessions in locations such as colleges or libraries. These are free for people with few qualifications, but if you already have qualifications such as O Levels, A Levels or a degree you will probably have to pay. In some parts of the country, if you are receiving social security benefits you may be offered a similar service by **Jobcentre Plus**.

There are also commercial agencies that offer careers advice or support which may be suitable if you have particular professional or executive skills. But they are likely to charge high fees for one-to-one coaching so you should make sure you know what they are offering in advance, and feel sure it will be value for money.

You will be able to find information on a wide range of agencies using an internet search engine. Another option is to contact **The Age and Employment Network** (TAEN) which will signpost you to one of their members (who should be committed to helping people over 50 find work). TAEN's website is www.taen.org.uk and their phone number is 020 7843 1590.

When you are over 50, you should think carefully about exactly what learning will be best suited to your circumstances. You will need to decide whether the time and money a course will entail will be worthwhile, taking into account how many years you plan to work afterwards and how likely the course is to improve your employment prospects. For example, if you are thinking about a degree or professional qualification that will take several years to complete, you should be confident, you will be able to find work in your new occupation. You also need to decide how appropriate a course is for you. The length of some vocational courses may be designed to cater for the needs of young people with little experience of work. If you have years of work behind you, a lot of the course could be irrelevant. It may be better use of your time to enrol in short courses designed to plug specific gaps you have identified.

If you are looking for work, training is an excellent way of gaining relevant skills and showing prospective employers you are serious about getting a job. However, you should be cautious about giving up job hunting or turning down work in order to complete a training course. Employers usually want to recruit people with recent work experience, so it may be better to take a job even if it's not what you're ideally after. Once you are working, you can carry on studying and start looking for other jobs.

On the other hand, there are some courses that will probably be worth doing while you're out of work. First, there are courses in skills that most employers will be looking for, like computer skills, written English and basic maths. Completing training in these areas will definitely help you find work. Second, there are full-time, advanced courses (including university qualifications), some of which you may not be able to combine with work. If you complete a relevant advanced qualification while you're out of work, employers are unlikely to hold your lack of recent experience against you.

You may find it is easier to get involved in training once you have moved into a new job. With vocational qualifications like NVQs you usually gain credit for demonstrating skills on the job, so it is often easier to make progress while in work. If you move into work while you are studying, you could consider asking your new employer to support you to continue learning once you have started a job. Another option is to combine learning with volunteering or part-time work, which will enable you to combine training and practical experience.

CHOOSING A COURSE

Once you start looking, you will find there is no shortage of training courses. The learndirect website and telephone service has details of 900,000 courses throughout the UK. You can find out what's on offer locally through learndirect, by looking for adverts in the local papers, or by asking at a library or nextstep agency. In many areas, a directory of adult learning opportunities is published regularly, for example by the local authority or a private company.

With such a wide range of choice, it could be difficult to decide what's right for you. The quality of teaching and facilities will vary. Courses are set at different levels, so they could be either too challenging or too easy for you. The style of learning varies a lot too, with some courses being very practical while others are mainly classroom-based. The course could be full-time or part-time, with tuition at different times in the week – or, if the course is by distance or open learning, there could be no formal tuition at all. You should also think about who else will be doing the course. Some people prefer to have quite a lot in common with their fellow students, while, for others, meeting different people is a highlight of learning.

You can get help making decisions from a careers adviser, for example through the learndirect telephone service or a member of the nextstep network. But you should also consider carrying out your own research. Colleges and learning providers usually publish prospectuses with details of the courses they offer, and these days almost everyone has a website containing full details of courses. **Ofsted** publishes inspection reports about each institution as a whole. You should also visit the learning provider, either at an open day or by arrangement, for an informal discussion with a tutor and perhaps to sit in on a class or ask current students about their experiences. Although it may take some time to research all the options via the internet, phone, directories, brochures and so on, doing some research will really improve your chances of finding the right course.

TYPES OF COURSES

There are so many different courses that it would be difficult to cover everything on offer in these pages. This section contains information about the main types of course and training that you will come across, helping you make sense of many of the options available.

First steps

There are a lot of courses aimed at people who have not been involved in learning for some time. They may be 'tasters' in particular subjects, or a general 'returning to learning' course. These often take place in local community venues rather than colleges. You may want to try a course like this to dip your toe in the water even if you are confident that you'll be able to move on quickly to a more demanding programme.

On the other hand, you may want to spend more time brushing up your basic skills, such as maths or written English. If you've been in a job where you haven't needed these skills it may seem a bit embarrassing asking for help now. But you won't be on your own – there are many people taking part in basic skills courses because they want to improve their maths and English.

There are also courses geared to helping people gain the key skills employers expect from people starting work. These are often offered to people receiving social security benefits by Jobcentre Plus. As well as maths and English, these courses will cover things like team working, problem solving, and computer skills. For more information on training provided by Jobcentre Plus, see pages 95–97.

Computer courses

Computer courses are often referred to as information technology (IT) training. These days being able to use a computer is a core skill that's essential for a huge range of jobs. The internet also helps with all sorts of non-work activities, from sending email to shopping online. If you are aged over 50 and have not used a computer before, you may find the idea of training on computers a bit daunting. There are, however, lots of courses aimed at people with no experience of computers.

Your local **Age Concern** may run a course that could be suitable for you as a starting point. As availability varies from place to place you should check with them directly (for details see p. 00).

If they don't provide a service themselves they may be able to suggest an alternative.

You may opt for a brief 'taster' course and then go on to explore the technology by yourself, perhaps using one of the many computer guidebooks available in shops and libraries. In this case, a short introductory course provided at a **learndirect** centre, local **Age Concern** or small training provider could be the answer. On the other hand, if you are looking for work and want to demonstrate that you have strong computer skills, it could be a good idea to take a more detailed course that will teach you all the main computer skills you'll need for most office jobs. There are two well-recognised qualifications, the European Computer Driving Licence (ECDL) and Computer Literacy and Information Technology (CLAiT). Both of these will teach you how to work with computer files, and about the internet and email, word processing, spreadsheets, databases and presentations.

GCSEs and A levels

GCSEs (General Certificates of Secondary Education) and A levels are the main qualifications most school students take at 16 and 18. They are usually in academic subjects, including English, maths, science, foreign languages and history. However, they're not restricted to school children, and adults often take GCSEs and A levels because of their interest in a subject, for example Italian or art. Most GCSEs and A levels are not designed to give you skills that are directly relevant to work and they are probably not the best option if the main reason you want a qualification is to improve your employment prospects. If you want to attend university as a mature student you do not need to have A levels (see the section on higher education on pp. 129–30). Some employers say in their recruitment material that they require a minimum number of GCSEs or A Levels. However, they will almost always accept equivalent vocational qualifications you have studied as an adult.

For more information about GCSEs or A levels, contact your local further education college.

Vocational qualifications

Vocational qualifications are designed to give you the skills you need to work in specific occupations ranging from accountancy qualifications to childcare accreditation. The standards you need to reach are set by each industry, based on their own requirements. You can take vocational qualifications either through a college (although this will usually include some work experience) or as part of your job, with your employer arranging for assessment, on-the-job training and off-site courses. There are several different types of vocational qualification, including vocational GCSEs and A levels, BTECs, and City and Guilds. The most common and well-recognised standard is the National Vocational Qualification (NVQ).

NVQs are administered by the Qualifications and Curriculum Authority. You can find out more information about vocational qualifications from your employer (or a trade union learning representative if you have one). Alternatively, for example, if you are not in work, contact a local further education college.

There are different standards of vocational courses, with a national framework so you know how difficult different courses will be.

NATIONAL STANDARDS FOR VOCATIONAL COURSES

Level 1 courses recognise basic knowledge and skills and are equivalent to GCSEs at grades D to G.

Level 2 recognises good knowledge and understanding of an area of work, and is sufficient to carry out many jobs. A full Level 2 qualification is equivalent to five GCSEs at grades A* to C.

Level 3 qualifications involve demonstrating the detailed skills and knowledge required to carry out a responsible job. They are equivalent to A levels and qualify you for university entry.

Levels 4 and 5 are other more advanced vocational qualifications, which are equivalent to higher education.

If you do not have any qualifications equivalent to the Level 2 standard (for example five O levels or grade 1 CSEs), you are automatically eligible for free tuition for any course leading to a full Level 2 qualification. This applies to any subject whether you are in or out of work. If you want to move straight to a Level 3 course, this may be free of charge too.

If your employer is arranging the course, they can access free tuition under the **Train to Gain** programme (www.traintogain. gov.uk or 0870 900 6800).

Higher education and professional qualifications

Attending university or another higher education institution (such as a specialist college) has become the main route into professional and managerial occupations. However, most people aged over 50 do not have degrees, as going to university used to be far less common than it is today, now that more than 40% of young people attend university. This does not mean that you will only be able to find good quality work if you take a degree or other higher education qualification, however. Your skills and experience are likely to be just as relevant to an employer as your formal qualifications. If an employer requires that applicants have a degree, without showing why equivalent work experience is not sufficient, this could be unlawful age discrimination (see pp. 3–4 for more information). On the other hand, there are some jobs where higher education or an equivalent professional qualification is essential, for example if you want to work as a teacher, health professional, lawyer or accountant.

You do not need to have A levels to qualify for higher education. Many further education colleges offer access courses which are designed for mature students who want to enter higher education. They usually last one year full time or two years part time. There are general access courses and programmes tailored to specific degree subjects such as sciences, social sciences, nursing, law and teaching. You can receive credits towards the courses if you have previous qualifications or can demonstrate relevant work experience.

The most common higher education qualification is a degree (eg, Bachelor of Arts or Bachelor of Science) and courses last a minimum of three years. Most people study full time but there are plenty of part-time options, the **Open University** being a well-known example. Obviously, a part-time degree will take longer to complete. Some degrees are in general academic subjects such as English literature, history or geography; others are vocational and prepare you for a specific profession, for example social work or law. Many people may wish to pursue a subject in depth simply because they've always wanted to know more about it; for some, retirement is or will be a golden opportunity to get back into education.

There are also shorter higher education courses, including higher education certificates, diplomas and foundation degrees. If you already have a degree you can take a one-year graduate or postgraduate qualification to convert to a new occupation (for example teaching or law). Many occupations also have their own professional qualifications. It is often possible to study for these while doing your job without having to enrol in higher education.

For information about undergraduate studies, contact **UCAS** (the Universities and Colleges Admissions Service). For more information on professional studies, you should contact the trade body or professional association for your industry (for example for human resources professionals the Chartered Institute of Personnel and Development)..

WHERE TO LEARN

There are almost as many different places in which to learn as there are courses to take. Some venues may suit you more than others: for instance, you may need to be close to work or your home; you may prefer a classroom environment; or perhaps you work better at your own pace, as and when you see fit. The following pages contain information on some of the main locations and should help you work out what would suit you, and your lifestyle, the best.

In the community

Training courses are available in a wide range of locations, not just colleges. You may find learning on offer in community centres, village halls, libraries, local charities, sports clubs or leisure centres. More and more schools are opening their facilities to adults living locally, and often you do not need to be a parent of children attending the school to use these facilities. Learning in local venues has the advantage of convenience. Many people prefer this option, especially if they have not taken part in formal education for a while.

Community-based learning is particularly suitable for improving your computer skills or taking part in courses where you can do most of the learning on a computer (see the section on distance and open learning on p. 132). learndirect has a national network of centres which offer computer-based learning in local venues, while many Age Concerns offer a computer desk where you can take a computer 'taster' course and then get on with your own learning (see information on p. 126). Other courses available in the community are often introductory taster courses to give you a chance to try out something new. You will often find that for more advanced or employment-related training you will need to travel to a college, especially if it's a practical subject where special equipment is needed.

Colleges of further or adult education

Longer or more advanced courses are usually offered in colleges. There are two main types of colleges offering learning to adults: further education colleges and adult education colleges. The idea is that further education colleges provided more work-focused and longer-term training, while adult education colleges offered courses unrelated to work. The government's funding arrangements encourage this split but you will still find there is a good deal of overlap between what is on offer at colleges of further and adult education. However, they are funded in different ways by the government and they could charge different fees, even for courses that appear similar.

Universities or higher education colleges

If you want to do a degree, you will almost always need to attend a university. The exception is open or distance learning, for example the **Open University**. You may be able to start a higher education qualification at a further education college and then complete it at a university. Some universities also offer courses that do not lead to higher education qualifications, for example through a department of continuing learning.

Distance and open learning

Travelling to a certain place at fixed times each week may not fit in with the rest of your life. Distance and open learning allows you to take control of your learning, using materials from the learning provider, such as study packs, CD-ROMs or access to websites. This option is different from just using a website or buying a book or CD to teach yourself. Providers will offer you ongoing support throughout your course, and often you will be accredited or pass an exam at the end. Some distance and open learning provision includes limited formal teaching at specific points during the course: a weekend every three months, for instance. The rest of the time you can study in your own home, or use a local centre where you have access to facilities and supportive staff. Distance and open learning is very flexible, but it does not suit everyone. You need to have motivation and discipline to build regular learning into the rest of your life. You will also have less of the interaction with teachers and fellow students that often improves people's learning experience or enjoyment of the course.

The best known distance learning provider is the Open University, but there are a wide range of other providers including learndirect and a range of charities and businesses. Commercial providers are not inspected by the government so you should make sure the organisation is reputable and you know the course you are buying is right for you.

The **Open and Distance Learning Quality Council** and the **Association of British Correspondence Colleges** both expect their members to reach minimum standards, which are listed on their websites.

Learning through your employer

Most employers offer training that they consider essential for you to do your job. Some employers also support their employees' longer-term training, particularly where this is relevant to their occupation, this may involve helping you develop your skills for another role, even if they're not required for your current job. If you work for a large employer they may have a written policy on what support they will offer employees who want to learn. Some employers will even support training that is unrelated to the job. If your employer doesn't mention training you should consider asking about it, for example at your recruitment interview or during an appraisal.

Employers may provide on-site training for you, or arrange for you to attend training courses delivered by a learning provider. They may support you to do a course you have chosen, for example by contributing towards the fees or giving you time off to study. If your employer refuses to offer you training that is available to younger colleagues, this could be unlawful age discrimination (see pp. 3, 5). If you are a trade union member, your union should be able to offer you help and advice about training. In many workplaces there is a designated trade union learning representative who will be able to help you access training in the workplace.

Your employer may be able to access government money to support your training. For example, Train to Gain is a new national programme which pays the costs of tuition for employees with low skills to participate in training. Under the scheme, employers need to provide time off for study during working hours, although smaller employers can claim the costs back.

Jobcentre Plus courses

If you are out of work and receiving benefits, you may be eligible for free Jobcentre Plus training (if you are receiving Jobseeker's Allowance you usually need to wait six months for entitlement). In some parts of the country Jobcentre Plus may also offer you careers and training advice. You can either receive training after joining the **New Deal 50 Plus** programme or separately in which case it is called **Work Based Learning for Adults**. The training will be provided by a learning provider on behalf of Jobcentre Plus. The training that Jobcentre Plus offers is often short term and focused on gaining the basic skills needed to find a relatively junior job. However, sometimes Jobcentre Plus provides longer-term training to gain higher-level skills. One of the training options available is support and mentoring to help you go into self-employment. Jobcentre Plus can also help with your training once you have found a job. New Deal 50 Plus includes a £1,500 training grant, which your new employer can spend on your training if you are recruited while on the programme.

For more information on training provided by Jobcentre Plus, see chapter 7. For information on self-employment, see chapter 9.

MONEY – TUITION AND LIVING COSTS

Most courses provided by public bodies such as colleges and universities now charge tuition fees that cover part of the costs of the course, with the government paying the remainder. The system for paying for tuition is very complicated, with different arrangements depending on the type of institution you attend, whether you are studying part time or full time, and your personal circumstances.

You will also need to have sufficient income to cover your living costs and the extra costs associated with studying (eg, travel, course materials, a computer). Before starting a course (particularly if it involves a big commitment), you should carefully think through the financial implications and budget for all the expenses. If you are planning to borrow money, you should also work out how you will repay the loan.

Further and adult education

Further and adult education colleges are funded in different ways by the government, so their arrangements for tuition fees can be different, even for courses that appear very similar. When you are considering what training to choose, it is worth thinking about cost, as well as the suitability and quality of the course. For adult education colleges, there are no national guidelines on the fees charged, so arrangements vary around the country. In the past many colleges offered discounts to anyone aged over 60 but in recent years this has become less common. Even though these specific discounts are disappearing, it is worth bearing in mind that the cost you pay is still subsidised by the government.

Further education colleges, on the other hand, are required to follow national rules on tuition fees. They will normally charge you fees for part-time or full-time courses, but your tuition may be free for two reasons. See the box below for details.

QUALIFYING FOR FREE FURTHER EDUCATION

1 If you do not already have qualifications equivalent to Level 2 (for example five O levels, or CSEs at grade 1), you are entitled to free access to basic skills courses or training that leads to a full level 2 qualification. People without qualifications who move straight to a level 3 course may have their fees waived at the discretion of the institution.

2 If you receive one of a number of means-tested social security benefits, you will be eligible for free tuition for any course. The benefits are:

• Jobseeker's Allowance

• Income Support

• Council Tax Benefit

• Housing Benefit

• Pension Credit (Guarantee Credit element)

• Working Tax Credit (as long as your family earnings are below around £15,000).

You may also be eligible if your partner receives one of these benefits on behalf of both of you. If you only receive Incapacity Benefit or the Savings Credit element of Pension Credit, you are not eligible for free tuition (but check to see whether you are eligible for other benefits as well such as Housing Benefit or Council Tax Benefit). Local further education colleges may offer free or discounted tuition to other groups, at their own discretion. However, this is becoming unusual because of funding constraints.

While you are learning, there are a range of options for paying for the costs of living and the additional costs of studying. If your study is part time or arranged through work, the financial burden you bear may not be too severe. If you are out of work and claiming benefits, in most cases your claim is not affected by participation in further or adult education. The exception is Jobseeker's Allowance, where you will normally only be allowed to enrol in part-time learning which does not interfere with being available to start work. Note that you can *only* do full-time training on Jobseeker's Allowance if Jobcentre Plus has arranged the course or if it has given you specific permission to take part because it will help you find work.

There are other funding sources to support the costs of tuition, taking part in the course and normal living costs. Your employer may support you, for example by contributing to your fees or giving you paid time off to study. You could consider taking out a career development loan (see p. 140) or you may be able to apply to a charity or trust for a grant or bursary. The **Educational Grants Advisory Service** provides information on the support available. If you are on a course that will lead to a Level 2 qualification, and you do not already have a qualification at that level, you are entitled to the £30 a week Adult Learner Grant. On top of these sources, if you still face financial hardship as a further education student you can apply to your college's Learner Support Fund. Your college will decide if you are eligible but usually grants are available if you are receiving benefits, are disabled, or do not already have a Level 2 qualification.

Higher education
The system for higher education funding changed in autumn 2006. Full-time undergraduate students in England can be charged tuition fees of up to £3,000 a year (in future years this amount will rise with inflation). Most universities have indicated that they will be charging the full £3,000. There are no rules on how much graduate or part-time undergraduate students can be charged, so the amount will vary between universities.

If you are taking your first undergraduate degree on a full-time basis, you are eligible to take out a student loan to meet the costs of tuition fees and living costs. Students of any age can take out a student loan for fees, which can cover up to the full costs of their fees. You can also take out a maintenance loan covering living costs, as long as you start your course before your 60th birthday. The amount of maintenance loan you are entitled to depends on where you are studying and your household income (25% of the loan is means-tested). The loan is a very good deal. The level of repayments are linked to your earnings and you only have to start repaying once you are earning over £15,000 a year. Interest on the loan is linked to the rate of inflation. If you stop working permanently, for example because you decide to retire, the loan repayments will be frozen (25 years after your course ends they will be written off entirely). Part-time students and most graduate students are not eligible for student loans.

You should apply for a student loan as soon as you have a provisional offer of a university place. You can apply online at www.direct.gov.uk or by contacting your local authority.

In some circumstances you can study in higher education and support yourself by claiming benefits, particularly if you are already receiving benefits before beginning your course. Graduate and part-time undergraduate study does not usually affect your entitlement to benefits. If you are receiving incapacity benefit (which is not means-tested) this will not be affected by full-time study either. You should, however, be aware that if you are receiving a benefit because of a health condition which makes you unable to work, attending higher education could lead to Jobcentre Plus reassessing your fitness for work. If you are working for more than 16 hours a week and have a low household income, you can apply for Working Tax Credit. Full-time students are eligible for means-tested benefits such as Income Support or Housing Benefit only if they have a health problem or disability, have a dependent child or are over state pension age. If you take out a loan for maintenance, this will reduce your eligibility for means-tested benefits, so you should seek advice on what financial option is best for you.

Most universities and colleges have advice services offering help with financial issues. For more information about benefits and tax credits, consult the www.direct.gov.uk website or visit **Citizens Advice**.

Grants are also available to contribute towards your living costs. *Full-time undergraduate students* with a household income of less than around £35,000 are entitled to one of two grants (depending on whether they are claiming means-tested benefits or not). If you are receiving a means-tested benefit, you should claim a Special Support Grant as this will not count as income in your benefit assessment. Otherwise you should apply for a Maintenance Grant. The maximum award for either grant is £2,700 a year (for 2006/07). You will receive the full amount if your household income is less than £17,500. If you receive the maximum amount, you will also be automatically eligible for a bursary from your college of at least £300 (often it will be considerably more). Bursaries and scholarships are also available to a wider range of students, at the discretion of the institution. You should enquire about eligibility at the same time as finding out about courses. You may also be entitled to additional grants if you are disabled, are caring for dependent children or have a partner who is not working.

Part-time undergraduate students can apply for grants up to a maximum of between £1,000 and £1,375 (for 2006/07). These grants are a contribution towards fees and the costs of learning. If your institution's fees are more than the fee grant, then you may be able to ask for extra help through the Additional Fee Support Scheme. The amount of grant you will receive is dependent on your household income. If you are single and have an income of less than around £15,000, you will receive the full grant, while if your income is more than around £25,000 you are not eligible for anything. The income thresholds are higher if you have a partner or dependent children, but your partner's income will be taken into account in the calculation.

Graduate students may be able to apply for grants, scholarships or loans from a range of bodies including their institution, a charitable trust, research council, current or prospective employer, or an organisation linked to their profession (including the NHS for some health professionals).

If other sources of funding are inadequate, all higher education students can apply for Access to Learning Funds available from your institution. They are often available for students facing particular hardship such as rent arrears.

Your university advice service or the **Educational Grants Advisory Service** is a good first port of call for further information.

Career development loans

Career development loans are available to support the costs of up to two years of vocational study in further or higher education, where another source of public funding is not available. Courses can be part time, full time or distance learning (although a small number of subjects are excluded). You can borrow between £300 and £8,000, although there are restrictions on what the money will be lent for.

These are commercial loans offered through three high street banks: Barclays, the Cooperative, and the Royal Bank of Scotland. However, you do not need to begin making repayments until after you have completed your course, and the government will pay the interest on the loan while you are studying. Normally you must begin repaying the loan one month after your course ends, but you may be able to negotiate an extra deferral period if you or your partner are receiving a means-tested benefit or tax credit (either because you are out of work or in work with a low household income). Unlike student loans, you will continue to be liable for repayments even if you stop working permanently, for example because of ill-health or retirement.

Self-employment

Many people dream of working for themselves at some point in their lives. Some take the risk and leave work, throwing their time and resources into a business of their own. Others come to self-employment because they feel that age discrimination is holding them back, or they might decide to go it alone after a redundancy. Whatever the reason, it is often the case that people come to self-employment later on in life.

This chapter looks at the advantages and disadvantages of self-employment, the sources of support available, and points to consider if you decide to start your own business.

ADVANTAGES OF SELF-EMPLOYMENT

Working for yourself can give you a flexibility that you may not otherwise have. Depending on the type of business you go into, you may be able to choose your hours, the way you work, and where you work. It can be an opportunity to make a living out of doing something you really enjoy, or to use your skills and experience to do the work you want to do, on your own terms and for your own profit and satisfaction.

A significant point for people over 50 is that age discrimination on the part of potential employers is not a barrier to you getting a position; if you've ever suspected that you've been overlooked for a job because of your age, this can be a huge plus. Self-employment is a route into work which does not depend on finding an employer who is willing to give you an opportunity.

DISADVANTAGES OF SELF-EMPLOYMENT

Starting and running your own business could involve working harder than you ever have before, for longer hours, and if you've put a lot of money into it, the risk involved if it doesn't work out can make it even more stressful. There is no guarantee of a regular income, as you would have with salaried employment, and you won't have the same rights as an employee would have, such as paid holidays or sick pay. Of course there is a risk that, no matter how well researched your idea is, it may not make enough money to be sustainable. Even if the business is successful, it may be some time before you start seeing a profit.

ADVICE AND SUPPORT

The financial risk and the effort of getting things started can be daunting but there is plenty of advice and support available. This chapter gives you an idea of the things you need to consider, but for detailed advice you could go to one of the following organisations.

PRIME

PRIME is an organisation which helps people over 50 become self-employed or start their own business. It produces a guide to finding the right business or self-employment idea, to help you get started. It can then provide support, guidance and training to help you make the most out of your idea. In doing this PRIME works with local partners, such as **Business Link** (see below) or other enterprise agencies, which provide free business support and advice.

Business Link

Business Link is the government's brand of enterprise agency. There are local Business Link offices in most areas, which provide free support, training and advice to people who are starting a business. There may be another type of enterprise agency in your area, possibly working under contract to Business Link, where the same kinds of services should be on offer. Any enterprise agency will be able to offer guidance on producing a clear and realistic business plan, research, legal problems and financial planning.

Business Link has a very useful website (www.businesslink.gov.uk) with lots of detailed advice and information.

Jobcentre Plus

If you are on benefits, you can get advice and support on starting your business from **Jobcentre Plus**. You should ask your personal adviser what help is available, emphasising your age as some programmes are only available to people over 50. If you receive Jobseeker's Allowance (JSA) you may be able to start your business on a test-trading basis. At the moment, if you are on Incapacity Benefit and want to test trade, you will have to switch to JSA. This means you can continue to receive your JSA for up to 26 weeks while you are trading. Any profits you make during this period can only be used for the business but at the end of the test period, if you continue to trade, you can keep any profits to use however you choose. This scheme gives you the opportunity to try self-employment with less of an element of risk if the business does not succeed.

Working Tax Credit

Once you are working more than 16 hours a week, if you are over 50 you are entitled to claim Working Tax Credit. This can provide extra income while you are building up your business, when your initial profits may be low. Working Tax Credit is paid directly by Her Majesty's Revenue and Customs on the basis of your projection of profits. For more details on Working Tax Credit, see chapter 12.

GETTING STARTED

If you're thinking seriously about starting a business, hopefully you will already have an idea of what that business will be. It could be a new product or service – something that fills a gap in the market – or an existing business idea but in a different location.

It might be that you want to continue doing the same job you already do, but working for yourself rather than for someone else. Many skills can be transferred in this way (for example if you're a mechanic or an accountant). You need to remember, though, that there is more to being self-employed than the service you are offering; you also need to be able to deal with financial issues such as tax and bookkeeping, cope with customers, market your business, and comply with regulations such as health and safety. Think carefully – and honestly – about your strengths and weaknesses, and where possible plug the gaps with training, in-depth research, and good advice.

A lot of people decide to go into business doing something they previously did as an interest outside of work, for example computing, arts and crafts, driving, photography, or selling goods on the internet. The same advice applies here: the gaps in your knowledge and skills may need to be filled with a course or expert advice. Above all, you need to be sure that there are enough people who will be prepared to pay for your product or service, and that you have the skills and experience to be able to reach those people.

WHAT TYPE OF BUSINESS?

The three main structures for operating a business are as a sole trader, a partnership (if you have a business partner or partners) or a limited company. You should seek advice on which option is most appropriate for you.

The simplest way of setting up a business is as a sole trader. The drawback is that you will be personally liable for the debts of the business, rather than the business being a legal entity with its own liabilities. This means that if the business does not succeed, your personal savings and any assets can be used to pay off the business debts, and you could face personal bankruptcy. However, as a sole trader, you keep all profit from the business.

Similar principles apply to partnerships. Again, the business does not have its own legal identity and so any liabilities are the personal responsibility of the partners. The way that shares of the profit are divided between the partners should be set out in a partnership agreement.

The main difference if you form a limited company is that it will have its own legal identity. This means that it is liable for its own debts and own assets in its own name, rather than liability being linked to the individuals who own or run the company. It's a complicated process, so you will probably need to take legal advice on the formalities of setting up and registering a limited company. Accounts must be audited annually and filed at **Companies House**. There must be at least one director and a company secretary, so you cannot set up a limited company entirely on your own. As a director, you may have to guarantee any loans to the company and so there may be an element of personal responsibility for the company's debts, but not to the same extent as if you operate as a sole trader. Profits are distributed between shareholders (people who have invested in the company) as dividends. You could be the sole shareholder, if no one else has invested.

An alternative to setting up a business from scratch is buying an existing business, or a franchise. The obvious potential risk in buying an existing business lies in the reason it is being sold. Make sure you investigate thoroughly – don't just take the seller's word for it. If it is being sold because it is failing, is there something you can do to turn it around that the seller wasn't able to do?

Franchises

If you buy a franchise, you are buying the right to trade under an existing name that probably comes accompanied by a corporate image and standard way of running the business. For example, you could run a high street business such as a coffee shop, fast food outlet or estate agency, or work as a plumber or driving instructor, under a well-known brand name. Your obligations to the franchisor will be set out in a franchise agreement with them. If you are considering buying a franchise, you may get the benefit of a well-recognised, proven business with an existing customer base, but the drawback is that you will have to agree to constraints on how you run the business, and the initial cost of buying the franchise is likely to be high. For more help in deciding whether a franchise is right for you, visit www. createproject.org.uk.

Social enterprises

Another option is starting a social enterprise. This is a business which is run to achieve social or environmental benefit, rather than with the main objective of maximising profit for the owners or shareholders. Profits are therefore usually invested back into the enterprise or given to the social cause that the social enterprise supports. An example of a social enterprise could be a business manufacturing goods from recycled material, or running an enterprise which provides services and employment to disabled people. One well-known social enterprise is the *Big Issue*; another, on an international scale, is Café Direct – the fair trade coffee and tea company – but most social enterprises operate on a much smaller scale than these. For more information about social enterprises, see the website of the **Social Enterprise Coalition** at www.socialenterprise.org.uk.

FINANCING THE BUSINESS

Not all businesses will require a large amount of money to get off the ground. This will obviously depend on the type of business and whether you need to pay for premises, equipment, staff, etc. If you're not in a position to fund the business entirely yourself, you will have to consider getting a loan or asking others to invest in your idea in return for a share of the profits. If you have savings or own your own home, you will probably be able to get a commercial loan. If you are over 50 and are having difficulty obtaining a loan from a bank or building society, you may be able to obtain a loan through **PRIME**. You will need to show that you have a viable business plan and also that you have already been turned down for funding by a financial institution – usually a bank. PRIME can provide loans of up to £5,000 to one person, or up to £10,000 to a business run by two or more qualifying people.

Alternatively, you may be able to obtain a grant from a government agency, or from a charity or trust; for example, there may be grants available for research in a particular field, or for a business that could help to regenerate an economically disadvantaged area. **Business Link** runs a Grants and Support Directory which you can use to search for any suitable grants schemes that may be available to you. You can search this through their website, or you can go to your local Business Link office for assistance in finding and applying for grant funding. However, it is important to be aware that grants to help start a business are becoming increasingly rare.

BUSINESS PLAN

The most important thing you will have to do if you want to set out on your own is to draw up a good business plan. This is something that PRIME, Business Link or another enterprise agency can provide assistance with. You will definitely need an impressive business plan if you're going to be applying for a loan or a grant. Even if you're not planning on getting external funding, preparing a detailed business plan will lead you to address all the necessary factors which could affect the success or otherwise of your business. You should include details of your market research on your competitors and potential customers, and evidence that you have accounted for all the relevant expenditure in setting up and running the business, as well as meeting all legal or regulatory requirements. You should also include a financial forecast showing how you expect the business to perform over the first few years.

OTHER QUESTIONS TO ASK YOURSELF

- Do you have all the necessary skills?

- Have you thoroughly researched your chosen area?

- Will you need an IT system? How much will the necessary software and support cost?

- If you are employing others, how will you administer their wages? You will need a payroll system.

- Do you understand your own legal responsibilities as an employer?

- Will you have the necessary insurance to carry on the business?

- If you are creating a new product, or a new brand, do you need to protect your intellectual property rights?

- Do you have all the equipment you will need?

- How will you market and publicise your business?

- Are there regulations in your chosen area that you need to be aware of?

- What will you charge for your services?

- Will your funding last as long as it takes for profits to come in?

- If you are using your own home, do you need planning permission for the particular type of use? Or if you rent your home or are a leaseholder, do the terms of your lease allow you to use the property for business purposes?

Your business plan should include provision for income in your retirement. You may not intend to retire for many years, but it is sensible to account for some kind of pension provision from the early stages of your planning. You should also consider what will happen when you retire. Will you want to sell the business, or train someone up to take over from you? PRIME offers a guide to pensions for self-employed people over 50 (ring 0800 783 1904).

Once you have set up your business, you will need to register with **HM Revenue & Customs**. This is for National Insurance and tax purposes. HM Revenue & Customs runs a helpline for the newly self-employed on 08459 154515.

You may also want to register for VAT, although you don't have to do this until your taxable turnover reaches £61,000. If you don't have to register, it might still be worthwhile doing so as you would then be able to claim back VAT you pay on goods and services for your business.

An organisation such as PRIME or Business Link can provide advice and guidance on all of these aspects of your business plan.

Volunteering

There are a number of different reasons why you might consider volunteering. You may have recently retired and want something productive to do with your time, using your skills and experience. Volunteering can help with the transition from work into retirement. Or you may be wanting to get into work, or to change careers, and would like to gain some useful work experience or new skills. As well as the benefits to yourself, there are obvious benefits to others, both to individuals and your community as a whole. Perhaps the most important thing is to choose something to which you can offer a real commitment. If you go into volunteering just thinking about what's in it for you, you probably won't be successful in fitting in with the organisation.

If you are finding that a lack of recent, relevant work experience is a barrier to getting into work, volunteering is one option to consider. People applying for jobs are often advised to include details of voluntary activity on their CV or application form to account for any gaps in their work history. Either way, as an end in itself or as a route into work, volunteering can be very rewarding.

EXAMPLES OF VOLUNTEERING OPPORTUNITIES

There is a huge variety of activity that you could do on a voluntary basis. Here are just a few examples:

- information and advice work, for example as an adviser at **Citizens Advice** or **Age Concern**;

- conservation work;

- teaching English to recent immigrants or refugees, or teaching adult literacy skills;

- helping at a day centre for older people;

- doing administrative or campaigning work for a charity or non-governmental organisation;

- volunteering over the internet, for example providing translating services for a charity based abroad;

- volunteering for a political party;

- driving, for example transporting people to a day centre or hospital;

- working in a charity shop;

- sports coaching at a local club;

- public service work such as becoming a magistrate or a local councillor (magistrates are currently not recruited over the age of 65 and there is a retirement age of 70 – it is possible that this will change as a result of the new age discrimination law);

- working in local schools – help hear children read or volunteering as a school governor;

- becoming a trustee for a charity;

- volunteering for a community group.

Many volunteering roles will provide opportunities for training. For example, if you volunteer as an adviser at a Citizens Advice Bureau, you will receive extensive training in areas such as welfare benefits, housing rights and employment law, as well as training in skills such as interviewing clients. This is where volunteering can really add to your CV, if this is what you are looking for. Another advantage is that it will get you into a work-based routine. This will hopefully make the shift easier to manage if you do move into paid work.

Some volunteering roles could lead directly to paid employment, either with the same organisation (although this is quite rare and you should not expect it to happen as a matter of course), or in a similar role elsewhere.

MONEY AND BENEFITS

The obvious drawback to volunteering is that you will not be paid wages for the time and effort you put in. You will usually be paid expenses, to make sure that you are not left out of pocket through paying for things like travel costs.

As long as you are only being paid expenses, and you are not paid more than the expenses you have actually incurred, this should not affect any social security benefits you receive.

If you are receiving Jobseeker's Allowance, you can volunteer as long as you are still actively looking for paid work and are available to sign on and attend meetings at the **Jobcentre Plus**. You will have to be available to start work at one week's notice, and to attend an interview at 48 hours' notice. There is no limit to the number of hours a week you can spend in voluntary activities.

Your Jobcentre Plus adviser should be able to help you find volunteering opportunities. They may put you in touch with your local volunteer bureau or centre to find a suitable placement.

You can also volunteer while you are receiving Income Support. The amount you receive will not be affected, no matter how many hours you volunteer. The same is true if you are claiming Incapacity Benefit. However, you should remember that you can be required to attend a medical examination for the purposes of the personal capability assessment. The assessment should not be affected by your volunteering, as long as the type of work you are doing cannot be used as evidence that a change in your health condition means it is reasonable to expect you to do paid work.

Again, there is no limit to the number of voluntary hours you can do each week. Volunteering is not treated in the same way as paid work and does not count as Permitted Work under the Incapacity Benefit rules. See chapter 7 for information on Permitted Work.

There could be a problem if you volunteer but also do paid work for the same organisation as Permitted Work while receiving Incapacity Benefit. The Jobcentre Plus could decide that what you have done as a volunteer should actually have been paid work, and you could be seen as doing more work than is allowed under the Permitted Work rules. This won't be a problem if you do paid work for one organisation and volunteer for another.

If you are taking part in a Jobcentre Plus programme such as New Deal 50 Plus or Pathways to Work, your adviser may be able to help you to start volunteering, as a way of improving your chances of moving into paid work. For more information about this type of help, see chapter 7.

Your rights as a volunteer

Discrimination

Unfortunately, volunteering is not covered by the new law on age discrimination. Unpaid work will be included within the scope of the law when it is undertaken as part of a training course, for example a work placement with an employer arranged as part of a college course. Organisations involving volunteers can lawfully continue to set age limits for their volunteers. It is possible that under the European law which led to the introduction of the age discrimination regulations in the UK, volunteers should have been included. Therefore this is something that might be challenged through the tribunal and court systems. If you are facing age discrimination in relation to volunteering, it may be worth taking expert legal advice to see if there is any action you can take.

As a volunteer, in addition to not being covered by the age discrimination regulations, you will not have legal protection against discrimination on the grounds of sex, race, disability, sexual orientation, or religion or belief. Of course, it will be good practice for organisations to have a diversity policy which is applied to volunteers equally as to employees, and if you feel you are being discriminated against you should raise this with the organisation.

It may be possible to argue that, although you do not get paid for the tasks you do, you are actually an employee rather than a volunteer and therefore you are covered by anti-discrimination law. You would have to establish that the organisation you volunteer for has a contractual obligation to provide you with work, and that you have a contractual obligation to do the work, which will be very difficult for most volunteers to establish.

Health and safety

The organisation you are volunteering for still has a duty to protect your health and safety, even though you are not an employee. If the organisation has employees as well as volunteers, they will have responsibilities as an employer under health and safety legislation. Even where an organisation is staffed only by volunteers, there will be a duty of care to protect the volunteers from being exposed to a risk of injury. If you feel that your health is being put at risk as a result of your working conditions, or that the workplace is unsafe, you should raise this immediately with the organisation.

If you do suffer an injury or health problems as a result of your volunteering, it may be possible for you to claim compensation from the organisation if they failed to take action to protect you. See pages 220–23 for information on employers' health and safety-related duties.

How to find volunteering opportunities

There are many organisations that can help you to find a suitable volunteering position. There may be a volunteer centre, volunteer bureau, or volunteer development agency in your area which will know about local opportunities, or you could go through a national organisation such as those listed below. They can help you decide what type of volunteering would be most suitable, give you some ideas and put you in touch with organisations that need volunteers.

Organisations That Will Help Find a Volunteering Role

Volunteering England – can provide details of local volunteer bureaux or centres and volunteering opportunities in England. See www.volunteering.org.uk or look in your local phone book for details of local bureaux and centres.

Wales Council for Voluntary Action (www.volunteering-wales. net) – can provide details of volunteer bureaux and volunteering opportunities in Wales.

Volunteer Centre Network Scotland (www.volunteerscotland. info) – can provide details of volunteer centres and volunteering opportunities in Scotland.

Volunteer Development Agency – Northern Ireland (www. volunteering-ni.org) – can provide details of volunteer centres in Northern Ireland.

RSVP (Retired and Senior Volunteer Programme) – links people over 50 to suitable volunteering projects through local groups (www.csv.org.uk/Volunteer/Senior+Volunteers).

REACH (www.reach-online.org.uk) – recruits volunteers with managerial, technical and professional expertise, to work with voluntary organisations.

TimeBank UK (www.timebank.org.uk) – a national charity which provides information to volunteers and has a directory of organisations which use volunteers.

www.do-it.org.uk – a national database of volunteering opportunities in the UK which you can search by the type of activity you want to do and by geographical area.

Libraries – your local library should have information about local volunteering opportunities.

VITA (Volunteering in the Third Age) – a project coordinated by the WRVS to promote volunteering in retirement. See the website www.v-word.org.uk for details on how to register to become a volunteer.

Alternatively, if you already know what kind of volunteering you would like to do, you can approach the organisation directly. See below for a list of organisations that recruit volunteers. This list is only to give you some ideas; there are many more organisations not included here which are looking for volunteers.

Procedures for taking on volunteers will differ between organisations. Some will have a formal application procedure, involving an application form and an interview, to check that you are suitable for the role. In some organisations, for example if you will be working with children or vulnerable adults, it will be necessary to carry out a Criminal Records Bureau (CRB) check on you.

ORGANISATIONS THAT TAKE ON VOLUNTEERS THEMSELVES

Age Concern – see www.ageconcern.co.uk/AgeConcern/ volunteer.asp or look in your local phone book for your nearest Age Concern.

Citizens Advice – see www.citizensadvice.org.uk/index/join-us.htm or phone 08451 264 264

UN – see www.onlinevolunteering.org

British Trust for Conservation Volunteers – see www.btcv.org. uk or phone 01302 388 888

Friends of the Earth – see www.foe.co.uk/press_for_change/ volunteer or phone 020 7490 1555

National Trust – see www.nationaltrust.org.uk/main/w-trust/w-volunteering.htm or phone 0870 458 4000

Samaritans – see www.samaritans.org.uk/support/volunteer.shtm or phone 08705 62 72 82

Cats Protection – see www.cats.org.uk/supportus/volunteering. asp or phone 08707 708 649

Dogs Trust – see www.dogstrust.org.uk/howtohelp or phone 020 7837 0006

RSPB – see /www.rspb.org.uk/volunteering/index.asp or phone 01767 680 551

Museums – check with your local museum

Amnesty International – see www.amnesty.org.uk/content. asp?CategoryID=10101&ArticleID=2397 or phone 020 7033 1500

Oxfam – see www.oxfam.org.uk/what_you_can_do/volunteer/ index.htm or phone 0870 333 2700

Crisis – see www.crisis.org.uk/page.builder/Office_volunteering. html or phone 020 7426 3875

Royal Botanic Gardens – see www.rbgkew.org.uk/friends/ volunteers.html or phone 020 8332 5000

Independent Living Alternatives – see www.ilanet.co.uk/id16. html or phone 020 8906 9265

Local sports clubs – check with the sports club that you're interested in

St John Ambulance – see www.sja.org.uk/volunteering/adults/ default.asp or phone 08700 10 49 50

WRVS – meals on wheels, etc – see www.wrvs.prg.uk or phone 0845 601 4670

DIAL UK – see www.dialuk.info/volunteer.asp or phone 01302 310 123

Local hospitals – check with your local hospital

Adult literacy teaching – see www.literacytrust.org.uk/database/ voladult.html or phone 020 7828 2435

Starting your own project

If you can see a need for some kind of community action in your local area, that no one else is meeting, you could think about setting up your own community project, involving volunteers. You can get information and advice about how to go about this from the National Association for Voluntary and Community Action (NAVCA), who may also put you in touch with a local organisation which could help. Visit their website at www.navca. org.uk, or call 0114 278 6636.

V<small>OLUNTEERING OVERSEAS</small>

There are also organisations that specialise in placing volunteers in projects abroad. Perhaps the best known of these is VSO (Voluntary Service Overseas). VSO is an international development charity that places volunteers with professional experience in voluntary jobs in countries in Africa and Asia. The placements generally last at least two years and so a great deal of commitment is clearly required. VSO recruits volunteers with expertise and experience in work areas including teaching, accountancy, business, and healthcare. There is an upper age limit of 75 for volunteers. You can find out more at the website www.vso.org.uk or by phoning VSO's volunteering advice line on 020 8780 7500.

Not all overseas volunteering placements require such a long-term commitment. Volunteering England has a list of organisations that arrange overseas placements, including short-term placements lasting as little as two weeks – see www. volunteering.org.uk/iwantto/volunteeringoverseas.

Planning for Retirement

When we think about retirement we tend to have a stereotype in our mind of giving up a long-term job, stopping work altogether and *retiring* from life. These days, however, this is probably the exception rather than the rule. To begin with, many of us move between employers several times in our careers rather than staying with a single organisation, so we already have some experience of 'leaving'. On top of that, it's more and more common for people who have given up a long-term career to do something else for a few years before stopping work altogether. And lastly, retirement has moved on from what it was: free from the daily grind, with an extra 40 hours a week that you once spent at work, your retirement can be a time of new opportunities, challenges and excitements.

This chapter looks at how to leave work on your terms. Not everyone is able to stop working when they want to, in the way they want to. But the more you've thought about what you'd ideally like to do, the more control you may be able to take, whatever the circumstances. This means looking at the employment options available, such as part-time work or going freelance. It also means putting some thought into your financial future. Whether you approach retirement with excitement or reluctance, you will always find that good financial preparation will really help with what is, inevitably, a major life change. This chapter covers options at work, and provides information on the key financial issues you're likely to encounter. The sooner you get around to thinking about these questions, the more likely you are to make the transition smoothly, and the more you will be able to enjoy the golden opportunity that retirement can represent.

THE TRANSITION TOWARDS RETIREMENT

It's useful to think about what you mean by 'retirement'. In the eyes of your employer, retirement is the process of you leaving their organisation. What happens next is irrelevant to them. From the perspective of the employee, however, the process the organisation calls retirement could be much lengthier, and more complex.

As an individual, you can think of your retirement in two ways. Either you can see it as a particular point in time – the day you stop doing paid work for the last time – or you can see it as a gradual process: a transition over time from working full pelt to not working at all. The retirement transition encompasses whatever happens on the way, and may include reducing your hours, finding another job, or becoming self-employed; on a less positive note, it may include a period of unemployment or sick leave. The transition might last a few months or stretch out over a decade. Or, indeed, you may decide that you never want to stop working entirely.

For some people the whole idea of retirement may seem rather irrelevant. For example, over their adult life many women mix lots of different jobs along with taking time out to look after children or care for relatives. In this case stopping work for the last time may not seem like a major transition, but rather one more switch in a changing life.

Retiring from your employer

If you are leaving an organisation in your 50s or 60s, people around you may think you are making the transition towards retirement. But that's for you to decide; changing jobs may have nothing to do with retiring. You might want to move for career development – for example, to take up a more senior role or to branch out into a related area of work – or because you want a fresh challenge. In this case you may see moving on not as part of the retirement transition, but as launching yourself into your second – or third – career.

Whatever your reasons for leaving, it's important to make sure you do it in the way that is most advantageous for you. This may often mean 'retiring' in the eyes of your employer. For example, if your employer is wanting to decrease the workforce they may offer older employees early retirement, with a generous increase to their pension, and this could well be a better deal than any voluntary redundancy payment available to younger staff. Or your employer may have a minimum age from which any employee can retire and draw a pension even if they go on to work somewhere else. In this case it may suit you to retire rather than resign. Of course, you might be better off deferring your pension until you stop working altogether. The best option will depend on the terms of your employer's pension scheme.

Phased retirement

Some employers are happy to allow older employees to make a gradual transition to retirement, while staying within the organisation.

Flexible working You and your employer may agree to change your hours, or the way you work, during your transition towards retirement. You might want to go part time, for instance. In this situation you would, of course, be paid less, and you would only build up pension entitlement in line with your new earnings or hours; however, it's a great interim measure for those who aren't ready to stop working all at once. Alternatively, if you're fed up with commuting, rather than with work itself, you may just want to adjust your working hours to avoid the rush hour, or work from home some of the time. Employers are under no obligation to change your terms of employment, but many are happy to accept flexible working. In addition, if you have caring responsibilities, from April 2007 there will be a statutory process for requesting to work flexibly (see pp. 238–41).

Moving sideways Another option is to move jobs within the organisation. You might be able to make a sideways move. This option tends to be easier in large organisations where there are lots of opportunities. For example, you might be able to move from a management position to working on a specific project, or you could move into a training role where you can share your expertise with others. In larger organisations there could be a training department, while in smaller workplaces you might be able to spend part of the week mentoring other colleagues. In the 1980s and 1990s some employers seconded older employees into other organisations, such as charities or community organisations, while continuing to pay them. This is now unusual as it was a response to the difficult economic climate of the time. However, if this option is on offer, a move of this sort could be really rewarding and possibly open up opportunities once you have retired. Moving sideways won't always be possible but it can work well, particularly if you have colleagues who would like to be promoted into your job. Employers can then benefit from retaining your skills while also being able to offer someone else a new opportunity.

'Stepping down' Sometimes employees can also remain with their employer but 'step down' to a more junior post. This is not terribly common, partly because it involves taking a pay cut, but mainly because it goes against the grain of many people's assumptions about work; normally people expect to leave their employer at the most senior point in their career. However, it may be an attractive option if you want to stop working very long hours, or if there are some parts of your job you enjoy and others that you can do without. Some people decide to give up their management responsibilities but carry on using their other skills. For example, teachers sometimes decide to spend more time in the classroom by giving up roles such as being head of department or deputy headteacher.

If you are stepping down it is extremely important that you check the implications for your pension, particularly if you are a member of a final salary scheme. If you are not careful, your pension could be calculated on the basis of your new lower salary. In many schemes there are ways around this (for example, entitlement can be based on the highest salary you reach within a set number of years before your retirement). Alternatively, you might need to freeze your previous pension accruals and start building up additional entitlement separately.

Working and drawing a pension If you take a pay cut, either because you go part time or because you shed some of your responsibilities, you may be able to start drawing your employer's occupational pension while still working for them. For example, you could draw part of your pension to supplement part-time earnings. This is a new rule, which came into force in April 2006 (previously you could not draw a pension and work for the same employer). If you have reached the minimum age for entitlement to your employer's pension, you should ask about this, although you should bear in mind that with most schemes the longer you defer your pension the better your annual income will be.

QUESTIONS TO ASK BEFORE WORKING AND DRAWING A PENSION
- Would you be better off in the long run by deferring all or part of your pension for now? This could increase your monthly income for the rest of your retirement.

- If you start drawing your pension will you also be able to accrue further entitlement? Check what impact any further accrual will have on your pension while working and when you retire.

Other options for a 'flexible' retirement

Instead of phasing their retirement with an existing employer, many people move to new jobs as part of their transition to retirement.

Moving to part-time work You can go part time at your own place of work (see 'Flexible working' above) but many people who want to reduce their hours or level of responsibility decide to move. Industries which already have a high proportion of part-time staff are among the most positive about employing people in their 50s and 60s – for example large retailers and high street banks. However, many part-time jobs that people move into after the age of 50 are not particularly senior or well paid. If you move into a part-time job you are therefore likely to have to take a cut in your hourly pay as well as the number of hours you work.

Instead of deciding to work part time as a permanent employee, many people making the transition into retirement decide to work on a more flexible basis. Here are a few of the options:

Freelance consultant If you have professional or occupational skills that are in demand, you might be able to work as a freelance, carrying out specific projects. In many cases large organisations hire back their former employees as consultants in this way. It may not be a viable long-term option, as after a few years people tend to find that their skills and knowledge become outdated and their contacts dry up.

Self-employment You may want to set up a business doing something completely different. This might give you the opportunity to turn a leisure interest into paid work or to try out a bright idea you've had at the back of your mind for years. Or you may just opt for self-employment while you're job hunting, if applying for jobs is proving fruitless. See chapter 9 for more information on self-employment.

Agency work Another flexible option is signing up with an employment agency. An agency will place you with an employer on a temporary basis from a few days to many months. Agency work can be very flexible in terms of hours and the duration of any single job. It can also be an excellent way of getting a permanent job, as being a temporary worker helps you get to know an organisation (and the organisation get to know you). However, agencies will only take you onto their books if they think they will be able to place you with an employer, and they will then need to match you to an available vacancy. See page 00 for a more detailed look at employment agencies.

More than one job During the transition into retirement it is quite common for people to mix and match their work, for example by being a freelance and working for several clients, or by doing more than one part-time job. Sometimes people call this 'portfolio working' – impressive jargon that just means doing more than one job! This can be an ideal way of balancing out different things you want from work, and building up a good income from lots of different activities. Bear in mind, though, that there is a world of difference between being a freelance professional with more than one contract and juggling several low-paid jobs to make ends meet.

Financial planning and deciding when to retire

Planning for retirement is about money above all else. Unless you have been forced to stop work against your wishes, your decision to retire should always be based on an assessment of your financial options. You will need to think about your pension when you think about your retirement date. This is because other things being equal, the longer you work the higher your pension income will be. This is both because you have longer to build up entitlement and because you may receive more to take account of your shorter expected retirement. The higher your pension, the more enjoyable and secure your retirement is likely to be, so it's an important subject to get to grips with. This section offers guidance on getting your finances into shape, and deciding when to retire.

Financial planning can be extremely complicated, and comprehensive advice can only be offered by regulated financial advisers. If you want detailed information and advice you should contact the **Financial Services Authority** or an independent financial adviser.

The rest of this chapter looks at the questions summarised in the figure below.

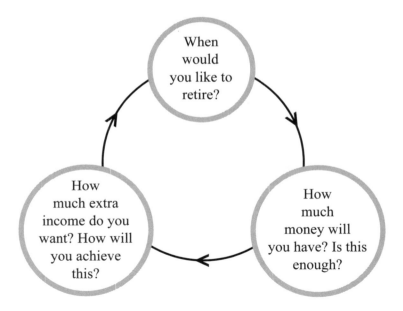

When to retire? You may have a very clear retirement date in mind, or you may not have given it much thought. For the purposes of financial planning you could work on the basis that you'll stop working at state pension age or at your employer's normal retirement age. Don't assume you'll be able to carry on working forever, even if you want to, because you might be forced to stop working against your wishes.

In the last few years expectations about when to retire seem to have gradually changed. Today younger adults still say they want to retire as early as possible. But as people get towards retirement, they are far more likely to say they enjoy work and want to carry on at least to state pension age. A growing number of people in their 50s plan to work beyond state pension age and in the last few years the number of pensioners in work has hit one million for the first time.

How much will you need? You should work out how much income you would ideally like and what is the bare minimum you think you could get by on. You can do this by drawing up a detailed household budget that takes into account how your spending is likely to change when you retire (for example less spent on commuting but more on holidays). Everyone's circumstances are different but pension experts say your retirement income should ideally be equivalent to two-thirds of your previous earnings, and if your pension is under half your earnings you may really struggle. This rule of thumb does not apply to people with low earnings (so, for example, if you earn under £9,500 a year your aim should be to retire on 80% of your former earnings), but the government will in any case top up your income through Pension Credit if you have limited pension entitlement.

As well as thinking about your short-term financial needs, you should bear in mind that your retirement is likely to last several decades, and your circumstances will change during that time.

From moving home to supporting your children or grandchildren, from repairing a leaky roof to paying for long-term care, there are likely be plenty of demands on your finances in the future.

Working out your future income The next step is to track down information on all the pension entitlements you've already built up, whether state pension, employer pensions or personal pensions (or a combination of all three). This information is available in pension forecasts, provided by **The Pension Service** and the providers of occupational and personal pensions. Forecasts predict your pension income, working on the assumption that you will carry on making contributions up to the scheme's pension age. If you've only ever had one employer, working out your pension income will probably be straightforward, but if you've moved jobs every few years you're likely to have lots of small pension entitlements. If you have lots of relatively small pensions you should probably ask for advice from an independent financial adviser about how much these pensions will give you in total, and whether you will be better off pooling them together in a single pension fund.

You should bear in mind that pension forecasts only give you a projection of how much income you are likely to have. The further away you are from retirement the less accurate they will be. As chapter 13 explains, the amount of income you can expect from a defined contribution pension may be particularly uncertain. This is because the income you receive will be dependent on the performance of the stock market and the price of annuities.

When you are working out your retirement income you will face a number of choices which could have a big impact on your income:

1 *Do you have assets that can contribute to your income?* If you have assets such as savings, investments or property, you may choose to treat them as a contribution to the income you

will live off. In particular, you might consider whether you could unlock capital you may have locked up in property. Moving to a smaller home or to a cheaper location can be an effective way of turning housing wealth into money you can spend. If this is not possible, you could consider buying an equity release mortgage. This is a financial product which pays you money in exchange for the lender taking a stake in your home and charging interest that must be paid when your home is sold. However, in the early stages of retirement you should see equity release as a last resort, since these financial products are poor value for money unless you expect to sell your home shortly. For more information on equity release, see the book *Using your home as capital* by Michael Philps and Cecil Hinton, or contact **Age Concern** for their free factsheet, *Raising income or capital from your home.*

2 *Do you want to take a lump sum from your pension?* Most occupational and private pensions allow you to take part of your pension as a lump sum at the point you retire. This payment is tax free (unlike your monthly pension income), although if you put the capital into savings or investments you may have to pay tax on your interest or profits. Taking a lump sum could be a good option if you want to untie some of your pension, either to spend in the short term (perhaps on a long-haul holiday, setting up a business, or helping your children with the deposit for a house) or in case you need access to savings in the future. However, the larger the lump sum you take, the smaller the size of your future pension income.

3 *What will happen to your partner?* The state pension and some occupational schemes have automatic rules about what pension will be paid to your husband, wife or civil partner if you die. If you are not married or in a civil partnership your partner will not receive a state pension and may not be entitled to a survivor's pension from your occupational scheme. With defined contribution pensions you need to decide for yourself

whether to buy a pension that will continue to be paid to your partner on your death. A surprising number of people with partners decide to buy annuities covering only their own lifetime. In the short term this will produce a higher income but, of course, it leaves your partner far worse off if you die before they do.

4 *Will there be annual increases to your pension?* With the state pension and salary-related pensions there should be automatic annual increases to your pension. These will protect you from increases in inflation, although they may not keep up with rising standards of living. For defined contribution schemes you will need to decide if you want to buy an annuity which rises in line with inflation. If you do not, you will get progressively poorer over time, although your initial income will be higher.

Topping up your pension income If you don't have enough money to retire at the time you hoped to, you have two options – save more or work longer. You can save more by making additional pension contributions over and above whatever arrangements your employer may make. This can be done by paying additional amounts into an occupational pension scheme (additional voluntary contributions) or by paying into another pension, for example a stakeholder pension.

Working beyond the minimum age at which you are eligible to draw a pension brings significant benefits. By delaying your retirement by five years, you could increase income from state pensions and defined contribution schemes by a half. The gains from remaining in a salary-related scheme for five more years may not be quite so high, but they are still substantial.

State pensions – you can defer your state pension while working. In exchange you will receive a higher monthly income for life, or a lump sum. See pages 193–94.

Defined contribution pensions – you will be able to make contributions for longer so your pension pot should be bigger. Your pension provider will also expect you to spend less time in retirement, so your pension fund will buy a higher annuity income.

Salary-related pensions – you will be able to accrue more years of service, as long as you have not reached an upper limit on pensionable service.

If you do not have much pension entitlement already, the situation is more complicated and you should seek advice before considering working longer or saving more. It may not be in your financial interests to save, because your additional pension income may lead to reductions in entitlement to means-tested Pension Credit.

The financial side of things may seem very complicated, but a little effort now can really pay off when you retire. It's never too late to do something about your finances, even if you're in your 50s and kicking yourself for not taking action earlier. Seek help and guidance if you need it, and with some careful planning you could be facing the future with confidence. And with your money sorted out, you can concentrate on the many other important elements of your future, such as friends, families, relationships, filling your days in an enjoyable and productive way – or just relaxing!

This book doesn't cover issues about how you spend your retirement, but there are lots of others that do.

Money and Work

This chapter focuses on financial issues that you are likely to come up against when working or looking for work. Although employers often take care of a lot of this – for example, National Insurance contributions – it's still important to know what's going on when it comes to your money.

EARNINGS

The National Minimum Wage is the minimum hourly wage your employer can pay you. It is currently set at £5.35 (from October 2006 to September 2007). The minimum wage applies throughout the UK to every employer. It covers agency workers, people working for a commission or piece-rate, part-time workers and casual workers. There are a very small number of exemptions, the most important being for people who are genuinely self-employed, genuine volunteers and students working as part of their undergraduate or graduate course. You have legal protection from being dismissed or disadvantaged for attempting to enforce your right to the minimum wage.

Whenever you're paid – whether it's weekly or monthly – you're entitled to an itemised pay statement which should list all deductions taken from your gross pay (that is, pay before deductions), giving you the chance to check that your employer has not siphoned anything off unlawfully or by accident. Deductions can only be made if they are required by law – such as income tax and National Insurance – or if you have agreed to it in your contract of employment or other written agreement. For example, you may agree in writing that your employer can deduct money from your wages to pay for equipment or clothing you use for work. If you work in retail, your employer can make deductions to make up for cash or stock shortfalls, as long as no more than 10 per cent of your gross pay is deducted. There are also special arrangements if your employer reduces your hours because of insufficient work.

If your employer makes unlawful deductions from your wages, or does not pay you at all, you can bring a claim at the employment tribunal. You must do this within three months of the date of the deduction or failure to pay.

You have the right to be paid the same as your colleagues in a range of circumstances. Under the Equal Pay Act employers are required to give equal terms and conditions to men and women when their work is the same, or where it is assessed as being 'equivalent or of equal value'; so, for instance, you should receive the same pay as someone doing a different job at the same grade in your organisation. You are also protected against being paid differently from your colleagues on grounds of age, race, disability, sexual orientation, gender reassignment, religion or belief. In these areas your rights are not spelt out in specific legislation on pay, but are covered by the general prohibition against discrimination. See chapter 2 for more information on discrimination law.

INCOME TAX AND NATIONAL INSURANCE

Most people in work are required to pay income tax and National Insurance contributions. These are usually deducted from your pay by your employer. There are, however, some important exceptions.

If you are self-employed you are responsible for declaring your earnings and making National Insurance and income tax payments yourself. For income tax you will need to pay by self-assessment. For National Insurance, you need to pay a flat-rate weekly payment (Class 2 contributions) and a percentage of your annual profits (Class 4 contributions). If you have very low earnings you will be exempted.

If you are over state pension age you are not required to pay National Insurance contributions, whatever your earnings. You should check that your employer is not making these deductions. To stop deductions being made you may need to request a *Certificate of Age Exception* (form CF384) from **HM Revenue and Customs** and give this to your employer.

If you have low earnings (less than £97 a week for 2006/07) you do not have to pay National Insurance contributions. Depending on what other taxable income you have (including the state pension) you might also earn too little to pay income tax. Your tax code will tell your employer what level of earnings you need to have before tax is payable.

Understanding income tax

For many people in work income tax is straightforward, because employers calculate and deduct payments directly, through the Pay As You Earn (PAYE) system. However, if you are self-employed or if you have a high income (more than around £38,000) you need to make a tax return using the *self-assessment* process. You may also need to make a tax return if you have several different sources of income, although HM Revenue and Customs could just adjust your tax code to take account of this.

A self-assessment tax return is a form which you use to set out all the details of your income and expenses. From this information HM Revenue and Customs can calculate how much tax you must pay. Each year you are expected to make a tax return for the previous financial year. If you want HM Revenue and Customs to do the calculations for you, based on the information you have supplied, you must submit the form by 30 September. Otherwise, if you do the calculations yourself, you must submit your return by 31 January. So, for the tax year running from April 2006 to March 2007 you would have until 31 January 2008 to file your self-assessment form.

You can submit your return online instead of filling in a form in writing by visiting www.hmrc.gov.uk.

The amount of tax you will be expected to pay will depend on your age and total income.

RATES FOR TAXING INCOME

Income above your personal allowance (and any social security benefit income) is taxed at the following rates (for 2006/07):

Income up to £2,150	10% (starting rate)
Income between £2,151 and £33,300	22% (basic rate)
Income over £33,300	40% (higher rate)

A fixed amount of your income is free of tax. This is called your personal allowance. For people under 65 it is £5,035 (in 2006/07). Most people aged over 65 are entitled to a higher personal allowance (£7,280 for people aged 65 to 74 and £7,420 for people 75 and above) although if you have a high income you are not entitled to this extra amount. There are also additional allowances for blind people, and for married couples or civil partners where at least one of the couple was born before April 1935. In addition, many state benefits and tax credits are not treated as income for tax purposes, including Pension Credit, Winter Fuel Allowance, Housing Benefit, Council Tax Benefit and Working Tax Credit. However, the State Pension, Carer's

Allowance, investment income, and occupational and personal pensions are all taxable. Pension income will usually be taxed at source under the PAYE scheme.

If you have complicated tax affairs, with several sources of income, you should strongly consider seeking advice from an accountant before making a tax return.

Understanding National Insurance

TYPES OF NATIONAL INSURANCE CONTRIBUTIONS

There are four main types of National Insurance contributions:

Class 1 contributions are paid by employed earners and by their employers. You are liable if you earn more than £97 a week and are aged below state pension age (although your employer still needs to contribute if you are over state pension age). The standard rate (2006/07) is currently 11 per cent for employees and 12.8 per cent for employers, although this will vary depending on your earnings and pension arrangements. You only need to pay 1 per cent on any earnings above the upper earnings level (UEL), which is currently £645 a week.

Class 2 contributions are payable by self-employed people who are aged below state pension age. Class 2 contributions are a flat-rate £2.10 a week, which is normally paid monthly by direct debit. You must register as self-employed with HM Revenue and Customs by completing form CWF1. If you have earnings below the small earnings exemption limit (in 2006/07 this was £4,465) you can apply for exemption from contributions by completing application form CF10.

Class 3 contributions are voluntary contributions payable by people who are not working or receiving National Insurance credits, including people who are living abroad. Unlike other classes of National Insurance contributions, they can be paid in arrears for previous tax years. Class 3 contributions can be very important for entitlement to the basic state pension. As they do not relate to earnings, they are discussed in chapter 13.

Class 4 contributions are payable by self-employed people under state pension age with profits over a lower profits limit (in 2006/07 this is £5,035 a year). They are paid in addition to Class 2 contributions. Liability is calculated as part of the self-assessment tax return and you pay every six months. The standard contribution rate is 8 per cent of profits.

Your National Insurance record is very important because it determines the amount of state pension you will receive (see pp. 191–93). National Insurance contributions entitle you to the following benefits:

- basic state pension;

- state second pension (entitlement is based only on periods where you are paying Class 1 contributions). Class 1 contributions in past tax years may also entitle you to state earnings-related pension (SERPs) and graduated pension);

- contribution-based Jobseeker's Allowance which is available for six months irrespective of your income (entitlement is based only on periods where you are paying Class 1 contributions). If you are not eligible (or if you are still unemployed after six months) you can claim income-based Jobseeker's Allowance if you have a low income;

- Incapacity Benefit (eligibility is usually based on recent Class 1 or Class 2 contributions);

- Widowed Parent's Allowance;

- Bereavement Allowance;

- Bereavement Payment;

- Maternity Allowance.

For the purposes of entitlement to these benefits you will be treated as having paid National Insurance if your earnings are over the lower earnings limit (£84 a week in 2006/07), but you do not have to make contributions until you reach the earnings threshold (£97 a week in 2006/07).

If you are a married woman you may not be entitled to National Insurance-based benefits. Up to 1977 married women and widows were entitled to pay reduced rate National Insurance contributions (also known as the 'married woman's stamp'). If you were already paying the reduced rate in 1977 it has been possible to continue on this rate provided that you do not become divorced or have a break in employment of more than two years. The reduced rate is currently 4.85 per cent of earnings above £97 a week. If you are paying reduced contributions you are not eligible for any National Insurance benefits, including basic state pension. However, you will be able to receive a basic state pension worth 60 percent of your husband's, once he is 65 and you reach state pension age. If you are still paying the reduced rate you should seek advice before switching to the full rate. If you are in your 50s you are unlikely to be able to build up a state pension worth more than 60 per cent of the value of your husband's so it is only likely to be sensible if you will reach state pension age before your husband does. For many women the main benefit of switching to the full rate is that you would become eligible for Incapacity Benefit.

If you are not working there are a number of circumstances in which National Insurance credits will be paid on your behalf, for example if you have been in training, unemployed or unable to work because of ill-health (you register for National Insurance automatically when you apply for social security benefits). Men over 60 automatically receive credits if they are not working. There are also special arrangements regarding entitlement to the state pension for people who are out of work and looking after children or caring for ill, disabled or frail adults (see p. 196).

BENEFITS AND TAX CREDITS WHILE IN WORK

A range of benefits and tax credits are available to you if you are in work. Some are available to all adults, while others are only available if you are aged over 60 or 65.

Working Tax Credit

Working Tax Credit is an income top-up for people with low and moderate earnings. Anyone aged over 25 who works for 30 hours a week or more is eligible. If you work part time (16 to 30 hours a week), you can claim if you have dependent children living with you, if you are disabled, or if you have recently found a job after receiving social security benefits for six months or more.

Low earners If you work full time and do not have children or a disability, you need to be on a low income to receive Working Tax Credit. If you are single you will receive Working Tax Credit if you earn less than around £11,000 a year (or £210 a week). If you are a couple the figure is around £15,000 (or £290 a week). The amount you receive will depend on your income, with the maximum for single people being around £30 a week and for couples £60 a week.

Returning to work If you have been out of work for six months, you are eligible for a higher rate of Working Tax Credit and can receive tax credits while working part time. This is a special arrangement for people over 50 and only lasts for your first year back in work. It could increase your tax credit entitlement by up to £30 a week. You can qualify if you have been receiving a range of benefits, including Pension Credit, Jobseeker's Allowance (JSA), Income Support and Incapacity Benefit. If you are out of work but not eligible for these benefits – possibly because your income is too high – you can also qualify provided that you have registered for National Insurance credits.

People with health problems or disabilities If you have a disability or a health problem, you may also be entitled to a higher rate of Working Tax Credit and be able to claim when you are working part time. However, as well having a health problem that affects your work, you also need to meet one of a number of other requirements. There are three ways of qualifying:

1 You are receiving Disability Living Allowance while you are working.

2 You move into work after having claimed a benefit related to your disability. The benefits include Incapacity Benefit (except for the short-term lower rate) and other benefits, as long as you are receiving a 'disability premium' as part of your payment (eg Income Support, Jobseeker's Allowance, Housing Benefit and Council Tax Benefit).

3 You have started work after 20 weeks or more of receiving compensation for being unable to work (ie, statutory or occupational sick pay, Incapacity Benefit at the short-term lower rate, Income Support, or National Insurance credits on grounds of incapacity to work). However, you will be eligible only if, when you return to work, your earnings are at least 20 per cent less than what they were before you had the disability or health problem (with a minimum reduction of £15 a week).

Children If you have dependent children you are eligible for Working Tax Credit, including additions for childcare, and also Child Tax Credit. The system is much more generous than for people without children and you will be eligible for some support even with quite a high income.

State pension

If you have reached state pension age (60 for women and 65 for men), you are entitled to claim your state pension, even if you are still working. Payment is not automatic but the Pensions Service should send you a claim form four months before you reach state pension age. If you are still in work and earning, it's probably a good idea to think twice before claiming this payment: the longer you defer your pension the higher the rate you will eventually receive – or the greater the lump sum you will be able to build up.

Pension Credit

Pension Credit is the main income-related benefit for people aged over 60. It has two components: Guarantee Credit and Savings Credit. Both parts of Pension Credit are calculated on the basis of your household income, so if you have a partner both of your income and savings will be taken into account.

Note that this section looks only at claiming Pension Credit while you are working. For full details of Pension Credit, see Sally West's *Your Rights* (see p. 277), available from Age Concern.

Guarantee Credit offers a guaranteed income to anyone aged over 60. In 2006/07 single people are entitled to £114.05 a week and couples to £174.05. You may be entitled to more than this if you have a disability, are caring for an adult with a health problem or disability, or have housing costs that are not supported by Housing Benefit. If your total income (including your earnings and any state, private and occupational pensions) is less than the guarantee level, you will receive the difference in Pension Credit. Income from most benefits is disregarded when making the calculations, but any savings over £6,000 are taken into account, on the assumption that you receive £1 a week for each additional £500 of savings.

Most people in work have incomes above the level for Guarantee Credit. However, the credit can be a useful top-up if you are working part time. For example, people earning the minimum wage (£5.35 an hour) who don't have any other source of income may be eligible for Guarantee Credit if they work for fewer than 21 hours a week. The disadvantage of Guarantee Credit is that it does not distinguish between people who are working and those who are retired. Since you have the same income guarantee regardless of your circumstances, anything you earn results in an equivalent reduction in the Guarantee Credit you will receive. The only exception is that the calculation of your payment disregards the first £5 of your weekly earnings (£10 if you are a couple and £20 if you are disabled). So, unfortunately, if you are aged 60 to 64 you should think carefully before deciding to look for a part-time job with relatively low pay. You may well find that moving into work hardly increases your income. If you are aged 65 or over, the situation is different because you may also be eligible for Savings Credit.

Savings Credit is only available to people aged 65 and over. It provides an additional top-up for income such as earnings, savings and occupational pensions (income from most benefits and tax credits are not topped up by Savings Credit). If you have an income below a set amount, Savings Credit provides an extra payment alongside Guarantee Credit of up to £17.88 for a single person and £23.58 for couples. This means working part time is more likely to be worth your while. For example, if your income consists of a full basic state pension and earnings of £25 a week, you could be up to £20 a week better off than if you were not working (depending on your housing situation and whether you are liable to pay Council Tax). If your income from earnings, pensions and savings is higher than the set amount, you may not be eligible for Guarantee Credit but can receive a top-up from Savings Credit until your weekly income reaches around £158 for single people and £233 for couples.

If you are eligible for Working Tax Credit, you should usually apply for this instead of Pension Credit as it offers a more generous top-up.

For details of how to claim Pension Credit, you should contact **The Pension Service**. You can fill in the application form (form PC1) in person or online. Alternatively, you can phone The Pension Service and give them a lot of the information over the phone, which will cut out much of the paperwork.

Other benefits while you are working

Depending on your circumstances, you may be entitled to other benefits while you are working. If you have a low income you could qualify for Housing Benefit or Council Tax Benefit. The rules for both these benefits are more generous for people over 60 (and particularly for people claiming Pension Credit). If you are working part time you may still be eligible.

If you have a severe disability you may be eligible for Disability Living Allowance or Attendance Allowance, which are not means-tested or dependent on being out of work.

MONEY WHILE YOU'RE LOOKING FOR WORK

The money you can access while looking for work will depend greatly on your circumstances. Other sections look at the money you can receive once you are entitled to a pension (chapter 13), if you have health problems (chapter 14), are caring (chapter 15) or have been made redundant (pp. 58–61). In all these cases your income is available whether or not you are seeking work.

Setting aside these examples, the standard source of income for people who are looking for work is Jobseeker's Allowance, the benefit available to people who are unemployed. If you are aged below state pension age and not working (or working less than 16 hours a week), you are entitled if you are seeking work, capable of working and available to start work. The standard rate of JSA is £57.45 a week (2006/07 prices).

Men aged between 60 and 64 are still eligible for Jobseeker's Allowance (and other benefits such as Incapacity Benefit). However, you should consider claiming Pension Credit instead, as it will usually be paid at a more generous rate. You should claim Jobseeker's Allowance if your income is too high to receive Pension Credit.

If you have left your job voluntarily without good reason, your JSA may be deducted for up to six months. You will not be entitled to claim for periods where you are still counted as being paid, for example if you leave early in lieu of notice or if you received redundancy pay at a rate higher than the minimum set down by the statutory scheme (see pp. 58–61).

To maintain entitlement to the benefit, you need to sign a Jobseeker's Agreement, which will set out the steps you will take to find work. You will then have to attend fortnightly meetings, where you may need to demonstrate evidence that you have been taking steps to find work. At various points in your claim you may be required or invited to participate in more intensive activities, in particular after six months on the benefit. For more information on support available from Jobcentre Plus see pages 95–97.

To apply for JSA you need to call the national Jobcentre Plus phoneline (0845 6060 234) or contact your local Jobcentre Plus office.

There are two categories of JSA – contribution-based and income-based. Contribution-based Jobseeker's Allowance is available for up to 26 weeks to anyone with adequate National Insurance contributions (see p. 182). It is a contributory benefit like the state pension so there is no reason not to claim. Most income and savings do not affect entitlement. However, if you receive an occupational or private pension of more than £50 a week, the excess benefit will be deducted from your JSA.

Income-based JSA does not have a six months cut-off. It is a means-tested benefit that is only available if you have a low income and little savings. It is available from the outset of a claim if you have inadequate National Insurance contributions to qualify for the contributory benefit. You may also be eligible for income-based JSA on top of the contribution-based allowance if this does not provide sufficient income for your family. If you have a pension income, this will be taken into account in calculating eligibility at the point the benefit becomes means-tested. However, while you continue looking for work you will still be eligible for National Insurance credits, so if you do not have sufficient contributions for a full state pension you should make sure you remain registered with Jobcentre Plus (see p. 95).

Pensions

Reaching 50 is often a prompt to start thinking really seriously about pensions and retirement income. Of course, it's never too early to think about retirement planning, but the decisions you make during your last ten or fifteen years in work are absolutely critical in determining the income you'll live on for the rest of your life.

This chapter explains how pensions relate to your employment and earnings from work. For more information on financial planning for retirement, see chapter 11.

The subject of pensions could be a book in itself ... and it is. If you want further information on contributing to or claiming a pension, see Sue Ward's *Your Guide to Pensions* (see p. 278).

THE STATE PENSION

The state pension consists of the basic state pension (worth up to £84.25 a week in 2006/07) and additional state pensions (state second pension and previously state earnings-related pension (SERPs) and graduated pension). Entitlement to state pension is based on National Insurance contributions throughout your adult life. The earliest age it is available is 65 for men and 60 for women, but remember that the state pension age for women will gradually rise to 65 between 2010 and 2020, so if you are a woman born after April 1950 you will be affected.

Date of birth	State pension age for women
on or before 5 April 1950	60 years
6 April 1950 to 5 April 1951	60 years 1 month to 60 years 11 months
6 April 1951 to 5 April 1952	61 years to 61 years 11 months
6 April 1952 to 5 April 1953	62 years to 62 years 11 months
6 April 1953 to 5 April 1954	63 years to 63 years 11 months
6 April 1954 to 5 April 1955	64 years to 64 years 11 months
6 April 1955	65 years

The government has also announced that the state pension age will gradually rise for both men and women from 2024. People in their 50s today will not be affected by this, but if you were born between 5 April 1959 and 6 April 1961 you will have a state pension age of between 65 and 66.

If you are not sure how much pension you will be entitled to, you should request a State Pension Forecast from **The Pension Service**. Some employers will give you a State Pension Forecast as well as a forecast of what you can expect from your occupational pension (this is called a 'combined forecast'). The State Pension Forecast will tell you how much basic and additional state pension you have already earned and the amount you can expect when you reach state pension age if you continue earning. It will also tell you if there is any action you can take to improve the amount of basic state pension you will receive. The forecast is made in today's money values, so you can ignore the effects of inflation.

To obtain your State Pension Forecast contact **The Pension Service** on 0845 3000168 or write to them at State Pension Forecasting Team, Future Pension Centre, The Pension Service, Tyneview Park, Whitley Road, Newcastle upon Tyne NE98 1BA. You can apply online at www.thepensionservice.gov.uk or by filling in a BR19 form.

Claiming state pension

You are eligible for state pensions from state pension age. It does not matter if you are still working or if you have stopped working. You will not receive payment automatically so you need to make a claim, unless you want to defer your pension. Four months before you reach state pension age you should be contacted by The Pension Service with a state pension claim form (form BR1). If you do not receive this you should contact them.

When you claim your state pension you should also find out whether you are eligible for Pension Credit, the top-up for people with low and moderate incomes. For information about claiming Pension Credit and working, see pages 186–87. You should also bear in mind that if you stop working you may become eligible for Pension Credit for the first time.

Deferring state pension

State pension age, currently 60 for women and 65 for men, is the minimum age for drawing your state pension, but you can choose to defer payment if you want to. This may be sensible if you are still working and have enough money to live on at present, because it will result in an increase in your future retirement income. The Pension Service can also give you a forecast of the likely effect of deferring your pension. When you do decide to draw your pension after a deferral, you will have a choice of receiving a higher weekly pension or taking a lump sum. If you choose the first option, the value of your pension will be increased by around one-tenth for each year you have deferred payment. So if you are a woman aged 60 and you decide to defer your pension until 65, your pension will be worth one-and-a-half times its original value. If you decide to take a lump sum, you will be paid the equivalent of the regular pension payments you have foregone, plus interest. Taking a lump sum is a particularly good option if you expect to be eligible for Pension Credit. This is because the lump sum will not be taken into account when calculating your entitlement, whereas drawing weekly extra pension will lead to reductions in your Pension Credit payment.

Deferring the state pension may not be right for everyone. If you are married or in a civil partnership there can be implications for your partner's pension, so you need to think through the consequences before making a joint decision. In the event of your death, your partner will inherit all of the increment or lump sum to your basic state pension but, in most cases, only a proportion of any additional state pension.

If you decide to defer your state pension, you do not need to take any action at all, because **The Pension Service** will assume you want to defer if you don't return the pension claim form. If you have already started to draw your pension, you can contact The Pension Service to stop your claim at any time (although they will take into account the pension you have already received when they calculate your extra payment). When the time comes where you wish to claim your pension, you will need to get in touch with The Pension Service and let them know. You will then have three months to decide whether you want to take an extra state pension or a lump sum; if you don't decide in this time you will automatically be sent the lump sum.

Entitlement to basic state pension

The basic state pension is calculated on the basis of the number of years for which you have made sufficient National Insurance contributions (including any National Insurance credits made on your behalf, see pp. 181–182). To receive the basic state pension in full men need to qualify for 44 years and women need to qualify for 39 years. The government recently announced that the required length of contributions would be cut to 30 years for people reaching state pension age after 2010. This will make it much easier for people to earn entitlement to a full basic state pension.

PROPOSED REFORMS TO CONTRIBUTIONS TO THE BASIC STATE PENSION – 2006

From 2010 the government is committed to making the state pension fairer and more widely available. In the 2006 Pensions White Paper it said:

We will radically reform the contributory principle, by recognising contributions to society while retaining the link between rights and responsibilities. This will be achieved by the following measures:

- streamlining the contribution conditions to the basic State Pension by reducing the number of years needed to qualify to 30;

- replacing Home Responsibilities Protection with a new weekly credit for those caring for children;

- introducing a new contributory credit for those caring for severely disabled people for 20 hours or more a week;

- abolishing the initial contribution conditions to the basic State Pension, so that caring for children or the severely disabled will build entitlement to the basic State Pension, without having to make a minimum level of contributions; and

195

- making a number of other simplifications to the rules for entitlement to the basic and State Second Pensions, and abolishing a number of complicated and out-dated provisions such as adult dependency increases and autocredits.

If you have been out of work because you were looking after children or you were caring for a sick or disabled adult (and claiming a benefit as a consequence), any *full* tax year you spent caring will be deducted from the number of years you need in order to qualify. This is called Home Responsibilities Protection and only applies to time off work after 1978. You should get Home Responsibilities Protection automatically for years when you receive either Child Benefit or Income Support because you are caring for a sick or disabled adult. You will need to apply for Home Responsibilities Protection if you spend at least 35 hours a week caring for someone in receipt of Attendance Allowance, Disability Living Allowance (at the middle or highest rate for personal care) or Constant Attendance Allowance. To make your claim, you should contact **The Pensions Service**. You can claim at any time up to state pension age in relation to years between April 1978 and April 2002, but for years from 2002/03, if your claim relates to caring for a sick or disabled adult, you must notify The Pension Service within three years of the end of the tax year for which you are claiming.

If you do not have sufficient qualifying years, your basic state pension will be reduced in proportion to the years of contribution you have missed. For example, if you only made the required level of contributions in two-thirds of the qualifying years, you will only receive two-thirds of the basic pension. If you made contributions for less than a quarter of the qualifying years, you are not entitled to a pension at all.

Topping up your basic state pension If you have not made sufficient National Insurance contributions during a tax year, you may be able to make up the gap by paying Class 3 voluntary

National Insurance contributions in subsequent years. Under the current system (if you will reach state pension age before 6 April 2010) this is likely to be in your financial interests as long as you have a mid to high income. However, if you are likely to receive Pension Credit when you retire, making extra contributions to increase your basic state pension could lead to your Pension Credit entitlement reducing.

If you will reach state pension age after 6 April 2010, you should seek advice before making any Class 3 contributions. At the time of writing, the government has said it will introduce legislation to reduce the contribution requirement for a full pension to 30 years. If you have already built up 30 years of contributions (including National Insurance credits and Home Responsibility Protection), making Class 3 voluntary contributions will not improve your pension. If you are in doubt, you should seek advice from The Pension Service.

If you are sure it is in your interests to make back payments on National Insurance you can be do this to six years after the end of the tax year in question. The cost of a full backdated contribution will be between £300 and £370 for each tax year (the amount rises annually). **HM Revenue and Customs** should write to you 18 months after the end of a tax year if they think you have not paid sufficient contributions. If you receive a letter you should check whether there has been a mistake, for example because you were entitled to Home Responsibilities Protection or National Insurance credits during the period. Be warned that for the tax years between 1996/07 and 2002/03 the government failed to issue any warning letters. HM Revenue and Customs will have attempted to contact you during 2004 if they believe you made insufficient payments during any tax year in this period. For these years you can make contributions at any time up to April 2009 (or April 2010 if you reached state pension age before October 2004), even if you have already reached state pension age and started to draw your pension.

You cannot pay Class 3 contributions for those years where you were registered to pay married women's reduced rate contributions. Nor can you pay voluntary contributions for tax years where you are in work past state pension age, even if you have not built up full entitlement to the basic state pension.

Entitlement to additional state pensions

Your National Insurance contributions also determine what additional state pension you are entitled to under successive schemes operated over recent decades, namely state second pension, state-earnings related pension scheme (SERPS) and graduated retirement benefit). The rules for additional state pension have varied over time, but generally they are based only on Class 1 National Insurance contributions. State second pension, which was introduced in 2002, is available to a wider group of people including people caring for children and sick or disabled adults.

You – or your employer on your behalf – can opt out of the state second pension by 'contracting out', which means you and your employer pay National Insurance at a slightly lower rate. This is permitted if you are a member of an approved pension scheme.

Unlike with the basic state pension there is nothing you can do to enhance your additional state pension with respect to previous years. However, the decision you take about whether to opt in or out of the state second pension in future could affect your finances. If your employer offers a 'contracted out' salary-related occupational pension which they will make contributions to, it will usually be in your interests to join this. In other circumstances it is rarely advisable for people over 50 to contract out.

PENSIONS PROVIDED BY YOUR EMPLOYER

Employers with five or more employees are required to offer you access to a pension scheme. However, pensions come in many shapes and sizes, with some being much more generous than others. They range from stakeholder pensions to traditional final salary schemes. Some pensions are run by trustees for your employer (occupational pensions) while others are arrangements between you and an insurance company (personal pensions) which your employer arranges for you.

You can also buy pensions direct from insurance companies without an employer's involvement. This is useful if you are self-employed or if you want to top up the pension offered by your employer with additional contributions. These pensions operate on the same basis as personal pensions arranged by your employer. As this chapter's focus is on pension entitlements linked to work, these products are not discussed but you can find out more about the products available through an independent financial adviser.

The two main types of pension offered by employers are salary-related schemes (which are always occupational pensions) and defined contribution schemes (which may be either occupational or personal pensions). A small number of employers offer 'hybrid' schemes which split the risk between employer and employees, by operating schemes with salary-related and defined contribution elements.

Salary-related pensions

Salary-related pensions, also called defined benefit pensions, pay you a fixed pension related to your earnings and length of service. The best known type of scheme is a final salary pension. This takes your final year's salary as the reference point for your pension. Other versions may base your pension on the highest salary you reach or the average salary over your whole career (revalued to take account of differences in pay over time). Your pension entitlement will be calculated by paying you a fraction of the reference salary for each year of your employment. For example, your scheme might pay 1/60th of your salary for each year of service, meaning that if you were employed for 40 years you would build up a pension worth two-thirds of your annual earnings. For further details you should consult the information on your scheme provided by your employer.

Salary-related pensions are usually viewed as the 'gold standard' for occupational pensions. However, in the last few years, problems with these schemes have become front-page news. Many employers have concluded that increasing costs, and unknown future risks, mean they cannot afford to retain a defined benefit scheme. A large number of employers in the private sector have closed their schemes to new members. Some employers have also increased employee contributions or reduced the benefits available. In the public sector, salary-related schemes seem secure, although for new members normal pension ages have been increased from 60 to 65.

Salary-related pensions are a particularly good deal for people in their 50s and 60s. For various reasons, if you join a pension scheme aged over 50 the chances are you will get out more than you put in. You will almost certainly generate a higher income than if you made identical contributions into a defined contribution pension. To compensate for this, however, you may find that there is an upper age limit for joining or higher contribution rates for older members.

In the last few years most of us have heard about employers with high pension liabilities who have gone bankrupt and been unable to pay their promises. To prevent this happening in future, the government has set up the **Pension Protection Fund** which will pay your pension if your employer becomes insolvent and there is not enough money in the pension scheme. If you have already retired (except for early retirements unrelated to ill-health), you will receive 100 per cent of the value of your pension. If you are still working, you will receive 90 per cent of the pension entitlement you had built up at the time of the insolvency. Annual increases are restricted to a maximum of 2.5 per cent and for people with high pension incomes (equivalent to £29,000 for a 65-year-old) there is a cap on support.

Defined contribution pensions

Defined contribution pensions (sometimes called money-purchase schemes) are schemes where you build up your own pension fund. Contributions are made into your pension and these funds are invested. There is usually some flexibility for you to make your own investment decisions, although the scheme will also have a default investment strategy, which is usually based on how long there is before you retire (often called 'lifestyle' arrangements). This means that if you are some years from retiring, your money will be tied up in investments which, though they may rise and fall in the short term, should give a high return over the long term. This usually means that the pension fund is invested in the stock market. As you near retirement, in order to safeguard your retirement income, your money will be gradually transferred into low-risk investments which are unlikely to lose value, but which will not have so much potential for growth.

When you retire, your pension fund consists of your original contributions and all the returns on your investments (minus the fees charged by the pension provider). Normally, when people retire they buy an annuity which converts the value of the fund into a monthly pension, payable for the rest of your life. You also have the choice of taking part of your pension (up to 25 per cent) as a tax free lump sum. In recent years the value of annuities has fallen, as a result of rising life expectancy. At the moment the highest annuity a man aged 65 could expect to buy would provide an annual income of 7 per cent of his pension fund (ie, £7,000 of income for every £100,000 of savings). The value for annuities is lower still for women because they can expect to live longer. There are other annuity options which further reduce your annual income. For example, you can choose for the pension to be paid to your partner if you die or you can decide to receive annual increases to your pension to take account of inflation. On the other hand, you may be able to get a better deal if you have poor health or are a smoker, because the statisticians predict you will die sooner. It's worth bearing in mind that if you delay retirement your pension income will be considerably higher. For example, if you delay retiring by five years your pension is likely to be worth at least one-and-a-half times its original value. People with large pension funds sometimes decide to 'draw down' income from the fund without buying an annuity, because this is better value. There are strict rules on how much you can draw down over the age of 75.

There are different types of defined contribution scheme, although they all work in roughly the same way. First, there are defined contribution *occupational pension schemes*. These are run by the trust set up by your employer (usually with outside professional advice). The scheme may be either contracted in or out of the state second pension (although contracting out is now rare) and it may include additional benefits such as life assurance or an extra pension if you retire early because of ill-health. Other defined contribution schemes are personal pensions organised by an insurance company, although your employer may be involved in arranging the pension and may make pension contributions. The two types of personal pension commonly offered by employers are *group personal pensions* and *stakeholder pensions*. You can also choose to buy a defined contribution pension privately with no involvement from your employer, for example a stakeholder pension offered by an insurance company. In terms of how these pensions work, and how they are regulated, there is no difference between equivalent products bought direct from an insurance company or arranged through your employer.

You may well have heard about stakeholder pensions when they were launched a few years ago. They are one type of defined contribution *personal pension*, with particular restrictions set down by the government. These rules place an upper limit on the amount a provider can take in administrative charges; they also require providers to permit small regular contributions and transfers to and from other pension schemes.

DECIDING WHETHER TO JOIN A PENSION SCHEME

Employers are pretty much free to offer whatever pension arrangements they like and they might only offer you the one scheme. This means you're unlikely to have much choice about the terms of your employer's pension. The main decision could be whether to join the scheme or to make your own arrangements privately. For people over 50 it's also important to consider whether you should make additional contributions, either by making extra contributions into your employer's scheme or into a privately arranged pension. These are both complicated decisions, so if you are in any doubt it is worth seeking expert advice, for example from an independent financial adviser. An independent financial adviser will also be able to advise you about the best options for buying a pension privately, such as which stakeholder pension to choose.

When you are considering whether to join your employer's pension scheme the key questions you should ask are:

- What are the benefits?

- Does your employer contribute?

- Will you also receive state second pension?

- Who is taking the risk?

Benefits

The main benefit is obviously the pension income you will draw when you retire – either through the defined benefits guaranteed by salary-related schemes, or from annuities purchased from defined contribution pension funds. But you should also consider what lump sum is available on your retirement and how much of your pension you will have to forego to receive it. Lump sums are very popular because they are tax free, but remember that they may be poor value for money over the long term. Your pension may also offer valuable benefits such as life assurance and ill-health insurance which on their own are expensive for people aged over 50.

Employer contributions

If your employer makes significant contributions it will almost certainly be worthwhile joining the pension scheme they offer – otherwise you will not benefit from your employer's generosity. Employers make contributions to salary-related pensions by making up the difference between the total contribution from employees and whatever the scheme is committed to paying. An employer may also make contributions to a defined contribution scheme, although many have been criticised for offering very low contribution rates. If you are a member of a trade union or involved in negotiating pay and benefits it's a good idea to suggest an increase to the employer contribution rate.

Alternatively, your employer may offer you access to a pension scheme but not make contributions themselves. This often happens with defined contribution schemes such as stakeholder pensions or group personal pensions. If your employer does not make a contribution there is not much to be gained from joining the pension scheme they offer, although it may make life simpler for you compared with arranging a private pension yourself. There are three reasons it could be worth joining, even if your employer does not contribute: first, they may have negotiated lower administration charges than are available to individuals; second, you can have your contributions deducted from gross pay before you have paid tax; and third, the scheme may include life assurance or similar additional benefits.

State second pension

The section on additional state pensions on page 198 explains how you can either contract in or contract out of National

Insurance contributions relating to state second pension. You should check whether the scheme your employer offers is contracted in or out. Most contracted-out schemes are salary-related pensions which are likely to be worth joining. For people over 50 it is not likely to be good value to join a contracted-out defined contribution scheme, unless this is the only way to tap into a generous employer contribution. Anyway, few employers provide schemes like this and where they are available, a contracted-in scheme is often on offer as an alternative. You should almost certainly avoid a scheme where your employer makes contributions that are only equivalent to the National Insurance they would have otherwise paid if you had been contracted in. For more details refer to information available from the **Financial Services Authority**.

Risk
Your risk depends on which of the two types of pension scheme your employer is offering. In the case of salary-related schemes an agreed level of pension is guaranteed. This means your employer shoulders most of the risks. To honour their promise to you they need to estimate how long you will live once you have retired, and how well investments in the pension fund will perform. They will then work out the size of contributions that need to be made to fund your promised annual pension. In the case of defined contribution pensions an agreed contribution is made each year, but there are no promises about the eventual level of the pension. When you retire, you will have built up your own pension fund, which is usually used to buy an annuity that pays a monthly pension for the rest of your life. While you are still working you shoulder most of the risks. If investments perform poorly you will have a smaller fund to use to buy an annuity, and since life expectancy is rising over time an annuity will buy a lower and lower pension for any given amount in your fund.

Other things being equal, it is better to join a scheme where your employer shoulders most of the risk. An employer is able to share risk between members of the scheme, such as older and younger employees, and run a scheme with a long-term outlook, balancing out periods of good and bad investment returns. If there are problems with the pension scheme, an employer may also decide to make higher contributions to make up a deficit (although they may close the scheme to limit further liabilities). On the other hand, there is also the risk that they will increase employee contributions or reduce benefits that can be accrued for future years of service. If your employer itself becomes insolvent, your pension entitlement is protected by the government-run Pension Protection Fund.

Additional contributions to pensions

There used to be complicated rules about making additional contributions to a pension (meaning paying more than the standard rate). These were removed in April 2006 and most people are now free to make as high a contribution as they like, so long as it does not exceed their total annual earnings. You can make contributions into your employer's pension fund, known as 'additional voluntary contributions'. Occasionally, employers may make additional contributions if you do. If you are in a public sector scheme you can 'buy' additional years of service to increase the proportion of your final salary that makes up your pension. Alternatively, you can buy a separate pension, like a stakeholder pension, and make contributions into this.

Pension contributions after your scheme's retirement age

There is increasing flexibility about when you can draw a pension provided by your employer. As with state pensions, pensions provided by employers are usually based on an assumed retirement age (often 60 or 65). However, you can boost your eventual pension income by delaying drawing your pension beyond this point. Under the new age discrimination legislation, employers will not be able to force you to stop accruing pension rights because of your age, unless they have evidence to show why this is justified to meet a legitimate business aim. So if you have exceeded your employer's normal age for drawing a pension, you may have a legal right to continue to build entitlement, in either a salary-related or a defined contribution scheme.

If you are in a salary-related scheme, you will be entitled to build up extra years of pensionable service (again, your employer can only stop you doing this if they can objectively justify it). Some salary-related schemes have been designed with flexible retirement in mind, for example Nationwide's average salary scheme. It is possible that your pension will also be raised to reflect the shorter length of your retirement (under the age discrimination law this is *permitted* but the government's guidance does not say whether it will normally be *required*). Bear in mind that there is an exemption in the age discrimination legislation which permits salary-related schemes to set a limit based on maximum length of pensionable service, as opposed to age.

If you are in a defined contribution scheme, you should normally be able to continue to build contributions and earn investment income, unless your employer can justify refusing this. It is possible that employers may try to refuse to permit late retirement in the case of older defined contribution schemes where an investment product matures on a fixed date. It will be up to the courts to decide if individual refusals can be justified. If you are denied access to a pension, you can still take out your own personal pension.

DRAWING AN OCCUPATIONAL PENSION

Pensions provided by employers operate on the assumption that you will retire at a designated retirement age, which is usually the same as your employer's contractual retirement age. However, in practice, retirement is much more flexible than this. In many organisations where the normal pension age is 65, the majority of employees retire before this official retirement age, while an increasing number of people are choosing to carry on in work after retirement age. Under the new age discrimination law, your employer cannot compel you to draw your pension at the scheme's retirement age, unless this can be justified with evidence. If you are a member of several pension schemes you may want to draw different pensions at different times.

Whenever you do decide to draw a pension you will have some choices to make. First, you need to decide whether to take a lump sum or not. In the case of defined contribution schemes you also need to choose an annuity (see p. 201). It is very important that you shop around rather than just accept the annuity offered by your pension provider. The decision you make will affect your income for the rest of your life. For details on how drawing your pension fits into the rest of your retirement planning see chapter 11.

Early retirement pensions

Pension tax law usually permits you to retire and begin drawing a pension from the age of 50 (this will rise to 55 in 2010). However, your employer's pension scheme may set a higher minimum age for pension eligibility, or may only permit you to retire below a certain age with special permission. If you retire early, your pension scheme will normally reduce your pension to reflect the extra costs it will bear from you retiring early. If you retire several years before your scheme's retirement age, this could significantly reduce your pension and it is unlikely to be worth taking your pension in these circumstances.

During redundancy programmes employers may offer early retirement packages on generous terms to people over the minimum age for the scheme. This used to be very common but is now unusual because it is costly in the long term. Offering an early pension rather than redundancy might potentially be age discrimination, if people aged over 50 receive more in additional pension entitlements than younger workers would receive as a lump sum.

Under the new age discrimination legislation there is an exemption which allows employers to offer more generous early retirement pensions to people who were members of a scheme on or before 1 October 2006; if you joined a pension scheme after October 2006 your employers will normally be required to reduce your pension to fully reflect the extra costs of early retirement. The government hopes that this exemption will enable current early retirement practice to continue for the time being. However, this will only be confirmed once relevant age discrimination claims have been heard by the employment tribunal.

Previous pensions

If you have contributed to a previous employer's occupational pension scheme or to a personal pension, you will normally be eligible to draw the pension at the normal pension age for the scheme. If the pension scheme still has your address they should be sending you annual statements anyway, and they should also write to you a few months before you reach the scheme's pension age to make arrangements for payment.

It is common for pension schemes to lose touch with their members as people move from one address to another. Previous employers or pension providers can also change their name or address, or be taken over by another organisation. The government-run **Pension Tracing Service** operates to help you find old pension schemes and establish your entitlement. If you are in any doubt you should contact them with details about your pensions.

It is possible to begin drawing a previous occupational or personal pension before the standard pension age. However, as with a pension provided by your current employer, if you do this you will receive less income than if you had waited until you are the normal age. In the last few years a number of financial companies have started marketing 'pension release' products to unlock old pension entitlements when people are in their 50s. These products should be approached with extreme caution, as taking money out of your pension will reduce the value of your income for the rest of your life. You should always seek independent advice before signing up.

Another note of warning: people aged below 50 are sometimes targeted by illegal scams which offer to 'liberate' a pension and turn it into a lump sum. People taking up these offers have ended up with a tiny fraction of the value of their pension or, in some cases, with nothing at all.

Lump sums

Under many pension schemes you can choose to commute part of your pension: that is, take a tax-free lump sum payment. In the public sector a lump sum is usually automatic, although this is beginning to change. A lump sum might be a good option if you want to make some big purchases on retirement or wish to make investments outside your pensions. However, taking a lump sum will reduce the value of your monthly pension so you should think carefully about what size of lump sum you really need rather than taking the maximum on offer.

Drawing your pension and carrying on working

Under recent changes to pension law, pension schemes can allow you to carry on working with your employer and draw a pension. This is a good option if you want to stage your retirement by shifting to part-time work, as you can make up for your lower earnings by drawing all or part of your pension (see p. 167). Under pension law, schemes are not obliged to offer this option and so far few have taken up the option. However, the government has suggested that it may be indirect age discrimination if your pension scheme refuses to let you work and draw a pension. It may also be discriminatory for a scheme to refuse to allow you to build up additional pension entitlement, even after you have started drawing your pension. In both these cases an employer would therefore need to be able to justify their refusal to offer you pension entitlements.

THE NEW AGE DISCRIMINATION LAW AND PENSION CHANGES

The new age discrimination law applies to any pension provided by your employer and to contributions your employer makes into a private pension. In some respects the law applies to pensions in the same way as to the rest of your pay and benefits. If an employer treats employees differently in a completely arbitrary way this will be age discrimination. For example, if an employer pays you lower pension contributions because you are aged over 50 without any reason this would be direct age discrimination – just as if they set your pay at a lower rate.

However, the way the age discrimination legislation affects pensions is far more complicated than it is with pay. This is because all pension schemes treat people differently according to their age as an intrinsic part of how they work. In many cases this is necessary and fair. For example, it is uncontentious that pensions should only be payable once employees have reached the minimum age at which they are eligible for retirement. The government has therefore included a large number of exemptions to the age discrimination law which pension schemes can use to maintain age-related practices. Pension schemes can also attempt to justify other practices, by showing with evidence that they are a proportionate way of achieving an aim unrelated to age.

Some of the main exemptions are:

Maximum ages for joining schemes – employers are permitted to set maximum ages for joining a pension scheme. If you are affected by this, you should ask your employer if they will make alternative arrangements, such as paying a contribution into a personal pension or increasing your pay. If they refuse it is possible that a tribunal would consider this to be age discrimination.

Variations in pension because you retire before or after the scheme's retirement age – your employer can reduce your pension if you retire early, or increase it if you retire late, to reflect the difference that your retirement age will make to the costs of your pension. If you were already a member of a pension scheme on or before 1 October 2006, your employer will continue to be allowed to offer you an early pension without a reduction that fully takes account of the extra costs. They will only be able to offer this to new members if they are retiring on grounds of ill-health. In other circumstances they would have to justify an enhanced pension.

Contributions for different age groups – salary-related pension schemes can set pension contributions at different rates for different age groups, if this reflects differences in the costs of offering the same service-related entitlement to people of different ages, so a member in their 50s might be asked to pay more than someone in their 20s. Similarly, a defined contribution scheme which aims to achieve a similar pension for each year of service, regardless of age, can set contributions that rise in age-bands. On the other hand, employers can also set equal contributions for all age groups, even if this leads to employees of different ages building up different pension entitlements or to cross-subsidies between older and younger workers.

Indirect discrimination in salary-related schemes – the government is anxious to preserve salary-related schemes, so there are a number of exemptions providing them explicit protection from challenges that they indirectly discriminate. In these situations employers would be exempted from having to justify their scheme. The exemptions cover linking pension entitlement to length of service, applying an upper limit on the number of years' service that can be taken into account, and closing a scheme to new members.

Health and Working

This chapter looks at the impact of health on your choices about work. It looks at issues facing people in work and options if you are not working.

Work doesn't always feel as if it's good for your health – especially if you're suffering backache from a day at a computer screen or have succumbed to the latest cold sweeping round the office. But most of the time, for most people, working helps promote good health. In recent years doctors have increasingly recognised this to be the case, even for people with particular health problems. For example, these days people with back problems tend to be encouraged to remain as active as possible, rather than taking long periods of sick leave.

Anyone who has been forced into early retirement, or has spent weeks or months job hunting, can probably vouch for the negative effects that tedium, frustration and loneliness can have on people's health. The simple acts of getting up in the mornings, leaving the house to get to work and socialising with colleagues provide the structure and stimulation we need in our daily lives.

THE DISABILITY DISCRIMINATION ACT

This section builds on the brief description of disability discrimination law on pages 26–27. In many respects disability discrimination law is similar to legislation outlawing discrimination on other grounds, including age. It applies to training and all aspects of the employment relationship, including recruitment, promotion, pay and conditions, dismissal, redundancy and retirement. Some of the legal protection is identical (ie, harassment and victimisation). But there are also real differences, so it's important to check your rights under each area of legislation. In some cases you may feel you have been discriminated against under both age and disability discrimination law. In this case you can consider making a claim under either or both pieces of legislation. The procedure for complaining about disability discrimination is the same as for other discrimination, described in chapter 5.

One noteworthy difference is that the other discrimination laws apply to everyone (young and old, women and men, black and white) while disability discrimination legislation only protects disabled people from disadvantage. It is not discrimination if employers treat disabled people more favourably than other employees.

The Disability Discrimination Act (DDA) provides people with disability with important legal rights. However, it should be stated here that the law is very complicated; if you are in any doubt about your rights and how to exercise them, you should seek advice from your trade union or a **Citizens Advice Bureau**.

The DDA has implications for other rights that affect your health at work. See the sections below on health and safety, sick pay and dismissal.

What counts as disability?

The DDA offers protection to a wide range of people with long-term health conditions affecting their day-to-day life, including many who do not consider themselves 'disabled'. For the purposes of the Act you are likely to be considered disabled if you have an illness such as cancer, diabetes, multiple sclerosis or a heart condition; if you have hearing or sight problems; or if you have a significant mobility difficulty, for example because of arthritis. You also could be protected if you have a mental health problem, including depression and other conditions associated with workplace stress. In all, around one in five working adults aged between 50 and state pension age are likely to be considered disabled. The Act also protects people who have recovered from a disability or health problem.

The legal definition of disability is a physical or mental impairment which has a substantial and long-term adverse effect on a person's ability to carry out normal day-to-day activities.

'Long-term' means a condition that is expected to last more than a year from the time it started. If you have a fluctuating condition it will count as a long-term disability if it is more likely than not that you will meet the criteria for disability in the future.

'A substantial effect on normal day-to-day activities' is usually taken to mean that when you carry out normal activities you need to take longer, or do them in a different way, compared with people without your impairment. 'Normal day-to-day activities' mean things like getting dressed, cooking, walking, sitting down, lifting things, shopping, or using public transport. It is not enough to show that your disability prevents you from carrying out specific tasks related to your job. If you have equipment or medication which reduces the effect of your impairment, the assessment is based on your capabilities without this support. An exception exists for people who use glasses or contact lenses, who are only protected if they still suffer impairment despite using them. **The Disability Rights Commission** publishes detailed guidance, based on past court decisions, about what should be taken as substantial impairment with respect to eight key areas of capability:

- mobility;

- manual dexterity;

- physical co-ordination;

- continence;

- ability to lift, carry or move objects;

- speech, hearing or eyesight;

- memory or ability to concentrate, learn or understand;

- perception of the risk of physical danger.

There are some important exceptions to the standard definition of disability. People who have been diagnosed with cancer, multiple sclerosis or HIV and people who have severe disfigurements are automatically considered disabled. People with other progressive conditions count as disabled as soon as their condition has any effect on their ability to carry out day-to-day activities.

For further information you should contact the Disability Rights Commission who offer advice to both individuals and employers about discrimination law. If it seems likely that you may have a claim they should be able to signpost you to a local source of advice. Their phone number is 08457 622 633 and their website is www.drc-gb.org. Note that from late 2007 the Disability Rights Commission will become part of the **Commission for Equality and Human Rights** (www.cehr.org.uk).

Direct discrimination

Protection from direct discrimination works in the same way as for other areas of discrimination law. Direct discrimination happens where a disabled person is treated less well, because of their disability, than someone in the same circumstances without that disability. It can never be justified by an employer. An example of direct discrimination is where an employer dismisses or refuses to recruit anyone with a certain health condition, regardless of circumstances. This is because they have applied a blanket policy based on their assumptions about a person's disability, rather than considering the individual circumstances.

Failure to make reasonable adjustments

The second way employers can discriminate against disabled people is if they fail to make 'reasonable adjustments'. If the requirements of a job or the physical features of a workplace put a disabled person at a substantial disadvantage, compared with someone who is not disabled, employers are required to take reasonable steps to adjust their arrangements to prevent the disadvantage. In most cases it is easy to identify reasonable adjustments that work for both the individual and the employer. A reasonable adjustment could be a physical alteration to the workplace, such as installing ramps or rearranging furniture to make an office accessible to a wheelchair user; or providing special equipment, such as a computer screen suitable for a visually impaired person; or it could be an adjustment to the method or pattern of working, such as a change in hours or place of work, for example to avoid rush-hour commuting.

A failure to carry out an adjustment that is reasonable cannot be justified. In some circumstances, however, an employer may conclude that it is not reasonable to make an adjustment, for example on grounds of cost (taking into account the availability of government grants), practicability, health and safety, legal restrictions on adaptations to premises, or if an adjustment would not overcome the disadvantage. But employers must go through the process of considering adjustments, including discussing options with their disabled employee.

If you have a health problem or disability it is definitely worth familiarising yourself with the law on reasonable adjustments. Unlike with other discrimination rights, this is not a right that you only need to rely on when things go wrong. You should be prepared to approach your employer on your own initiative with ideas for adjustments whenever your health or work arrangements change, or simply if you think of something that will help you manage your health and work. Discussions about adjustments are routine and can usually be settled to everyone's satisfaction. This is different from other complaints about discrimination which can be confrontational and are often seen as a last resort.

If your employer knows about your health condition they should also ask you about adjustments. Employers are advised in most circumstances to treat people as disabled either if they say they are, or if there is evidence that they have a significant health problem. For example, the **Disability Rights Commission** advises employers to assume people have a disability if they need to take sick leave for more than six weeks or for a series of spells totalling four weeks. However, if there is disagreement, the question of whether you count as disabled for the purposes of the Act can only be finally decided on a case-by-case basis by the employment tribunal.

Disability-related discrimination

Employers cannot treat disabled people less favourably for reasons related to disability than they would treat other people to whom the reason does not apply, unless they can justify this treatment. This form of discrimination is different from direct discrimination because the cause of discrimination is a reason related to disability, rather than the disability itself. For example, if an employer automatically disciplines anyone who is absent for more than four months this would be likely to disadvantage disabled people, even though the rule does not treat them differently directly on grounds of their disability.

Unlike with direct discrimination or failure to make reasonable adjustments, employers can justify disability-related discrimination so long as they have good reasons. For example, if there was no prospect of a disabled person returning to work after a long period of sickness absence their employer could justify dismissing the employee, even though the reason is related to disability. Justification is only possible if an employer can show that the reason for their action is material to the circumstances and substantial. The Code of Practice to the DDA gives the example of a carpet fitter with severe back pain who is unable to bend over and therefore unable to fit carpets. If he were to be dismissed, or denied a job as a carpet fitter, the reason would be because he was unable to fit carpets, and so this would be disability-related discrimination. In this situation the employer could show that the discrimination was justified, as the reason for the discrimination is material to the circumstances and is a substantial reason; that is, the person would be unable to carry out the job for a reason related to their disability.

However, employers also need to take account of their duty to make reasonable adjustments; if there is a reasonable adjustment that could be made, it is never justifiable for an employer to fail to make it. An employer who fails to make reasonable adjustments will also be guilty of disability-related discrimination, unless they can show that, even if the adjustment had been made, they would have still been justified in behaving as they did.

Harassment and victimisation
The law on harassment and victimisation is more or less the same under disability and age discrimination legislation.

Harassment is conduct related to a person's disability that has the purpose or effect of violating the disabled person's dignity or of creating an intimidating, hostile, degrading, humiliating or offensive environment.

Victimisation is unfavourable treatment against someone who has tried to exercise their rights under the Act, or against others who support them, for example by being a witness.

HEALTH, SAFETY AND WELL-BEING AT WORK

Your employer has legal responsibilities for protecting your health, safety and well-being at work. In the past these duties have been associated with preventing industrial accidents and diseases in occupations such as manufacturing and construction. But health and safety law nowadays also requires employers to ensure that you are able to work in a healthy way in modern office environments. This means, for example, providing appropriate equipment and lighting to prevent back pain, repetitive strain injury or vision problems. Employers are also responsible for protecting your mental health. So an employer could be held responsible if you have a mental health problem that was directly linked to a stressful workload or the work environment.

Although the law requires employers to ensure, as far as is reasonably practicable, the health, safety and welfare of employees, this does not mean that every risk must be removed or that an employer will automatically be liable if you become ill because of work. What it does mean is that your employer has a duty to identify, understand and manage health risks. Employers' responsibilities for assessing risk are to their employees as individuals, so they should take into account factors such as your age, health and capability, rather than assume that all employees are the same. Employers should assess your work environment to ensure that risks are reduced. For example, if you use a computer the risk assessment should include ensuring that you have an appropriate display unit, lighting, workstation and seating. Your employer should also consider the way you work, for example by providing safety training if you lift heavy weights or adjusting your working pattern if it is placing unreasonable pressure on you.

If you become ill or have an accident because of work, you can claim personal injury compensation from your employer if you are able to show that they were liable for the accident. All employers are required to have liability insurance to cover the costs of claims. The courts will find your employer liable if they did not carry out a correct risk assessment and take reasonable steps to eliminate the risks identified, and if this failure caused your accident or illness. Even if your employer is not liable, you may be eligible for a payment if they have accident insurance.

Good employers are increasingly recognising that the most effective way of complying with their legal responsibilities is to take action to positively support good health, rather than to simply minimise the risk of illness or accident. Supporting employee health usually reduces days lost to sick leave and improves the quality of people's work, as well as minimising the risk of compensation payments. So, as well as addressing specific health risks, your employer may offer a range of health-related support such as free gym membership or healthy eating options in the staff canteen.

Whatever employers do, sustaining good health is, of course, primarily down to the individual. Workplace health issues should not be thought of as isolated issues, but as just one part of your overall health and well-being. You will be familiar with most of the important ways of maintaining your health: not smoking, taking regular exercise, having a balanced diet including lots of fruit and vegetables, drinking plenty of water, and limiting your consumption of alcohol. There are also other factors that are linked to good health, which are more directly related to working life. They include structured activity, feeling in control of things, and 'positive mental attitude'. Of course, these are not things that everyone can achieve all of the time, but it's worth bearing them in mind if you're thinking about how your working conditions could be improved, or considering options for changing jobs or retiring.

If you develop a health problem or disability

Many employers provide support to employees who become unwell while at work. Usually this is motivated by both a genuine concern for their employees' welfare and by financial considerations – it costs employers a lot of money to cover sickness absence or to recruit replacements for workers who have to leave.

If you are ill for more than a week or so, your employer may contact you to see if there are ways they can help you return to work. This is particularly likely if it is not clear how long you will be unwell or if you are taking longer to recover than would normally be expected for someone with your health condition. They may offer you support with rehabilitation, for example physiotherapy following an accident, or they could suggest a phased return to work, where you begin by working part time. They may also ask if they can refer you to a doctor or other health specialist who is an expert at helping people return to work after illness. Large organisations may have occupational health or rehabilitation specialists, with responsibility for helping employees make successful returns to work. The level of support will depend very much on your employer, but at the very least they will probably want to remain in regular touch with you while you are on sick leave to find out about your progress.

Some people may feel that being contacted by their employer when they're unwell is an unnecessary and inappropriate intrusion – they worry it means that their employer does not believe they are really ill. However, in almost all cases when employers contact employees and offer help they have good intentions.

If you develop a long-term health condition or disability (whether or not you need to take sick leave), your employer may have responsibilities under the Disability Discrimination Act to make reasonable adjustments as discussed above. They should contact you to ask you about this in the event that a problem develops, but you can also raise the issue yourself. Reasonable adjustments could include provision of specialist equipment, shifting to part-time work or varying your hours (perhaps as a temporary arrangement after sick leave to help you make a gradual move back). Even if you do not count as disabled for the purposes of the DDA, your employer still needs to take your health into account when looking at health and safety risks in the workplace. Poor health may mean they take extra steps to prevent safety risks, such as providing you with a special chair if you have back pain.

In the past some employers have tried to use health and safety legislation as a way around their responsibilities under the DDA. Employers are, however, required to comply with both sets of legislation, so if your employer believes that your health condition or disability means there are unacceptable health risks involved with you carrying out a particular job, they must consider making a reasonable adjustment. For example, they could redesign the activity or role so that it is safe for you to do, or transfer you to another position. Employers are not allowed to have blanket policies relating to everyone with a certain health condition, so you should always be assessed on your individual circumstances and the particular requirements of your job. If you are aware of all the risks and are prepared to accept them, and if these risks affect only you and no other colleagues, then your employer should take your views about the risk into account.

HEALTH-RELATED DISMISSAL AND RETIREMENT

A dismissal includes any situation where your employer requires you to give up your job. For people over 50, health-related dismissals are often described as 'ill-health retirement'. Ill-health retirement can also be voluntary, where it is instigated by you or is by mutual agreement. For the purposes of employment law voluntary retirement on grounds of illness is viewed as resigning from your job.

Ill-health retirement

The key feature of ill-health retirement, whether it is compulsory or voluntary, is that it involves your employer agreeing to pay you a pension prior to the normal pension age for your occupational pension scheme. While this sounds good, be aware that your employer may reduce your pension to reflect the longer period of your retirement, with the result that the overall lifetime cost of your pension is the same. But often, as part of special arrangements for employees with health problems, employers will pay you the full pension you would have expected to receive at their normal retirement age.

It is the responsibility of your employer and pension scheme to decide whether you qualify for an ill-health pension. They are expected to consider what prospect there is of you being able to continue in work, and what reasonable adjustments could be made under the DDA to facilitate your return. For example, they should consider whether your job could be changed or whether you could be redeployed.

Your employer is expected to consult you during this process, and in most cases both parties will agree about the best option. However, it is possible that you will disagree. If you want to stay in work but your employer wants you to retire, you can still be dismissed (see p. 219). If you want to retire but your employer wants you to stay in work, you have limited options. You could try to carry on in work on the basis proposed by your employer for a trial period, or you could suggest getting independent medical advice. However, ultimately it is the employer's decision whether to pay you a pension. If you think that other employees in similar circumstances are being treated differently, you might be able to claim that you have been discriminated against on grounds such as your age, race or gender.

Health-related dismissal

Your employer can only dismiss you on grounds of ill-health for sound, objective reasons. This means they should always discuss the situation with you and consider the individual circumstances of your case. They may ask you if they can obtain additional medical information, either from your own doctor or by arranging for you to see a doctor they have appointed. If you are at risk of losing your job because of a health problem, you are likely to count as disabled for the purposes of the Discrimination Disability Act. In this case you can only be lawfully dismissed if your employer has already made reasonable adjustments or if they conclude that there are no adjustments that would be reasonable in the circumstances. For example ,they could consider giving you unpaid disability leave rather than dismissing you.

There are several reasons why you may be at risk of being dismissed because of ill-health. Your health condition may mean that you need to take *long-term sickness* leave. If your employer concludes that there is little or no prospect of you returning to work, or that they can no longer afford to keep your post open, they may dismiss you. Their decision may be based on a standard company policy on length of absence or be taken on a case-by-case basis. It is also worth noting that your employer may take disciplinary action with the aim of dismissing you if they believe you are taking long-term sick leave when you do not have a serious health problem.

It is also possible for an employer to dismiss you on health grounds while you are still attending work, although this is fairly unusual. Your employer can dismiss you on grounds of *capability* (where your health condition means you are no longer able to carry out your duties to an acceptable standard), *health and safety* (where your health condition means it is unsafe for you to do the job) or for *disciplinary* reasons (eg, if your behaviour is inappropriate due to a mental health problem).

In these circumstances your employer should again consider making reasonable adjustments before dismissing you. For example, they should consider changing your job or offering you another one.

Employers are required to follow minimum procedures when considering taking disciplinary action against an employee, or when dismissing them, even when there is no disciplinary action involved. This means they must notify you in writing, hold a meeting to give you a chance to respond, and give you the right to appeal at a subsequent meeting. All employers are expected to follow this procedure as a minimum, although large organisations may have a more detailed procedure. See pages 52–3 for more information on the disciplinary and dismissal procedure.

If you are aged either over 65 or your employer's mandatory retirement age (whichever is higher), the situation is different because the law says your employer can automatically dismiss you on grounds of retirement (as long as they follow the correct procedure). However, the law on age discrimination does not exempt employers from responsibilities under the DDA. So if you think you are being forced to retire simply because you have a health problem, you may be able to make a complaint of disability discrimination. Your employer also has a continuing duty to consider reasonable adjustments, even if you are over 65.

SICK PAY

The majority of sickness absence is routine and lasts no more than a few days. However, if you develop a serious health problem you may need to stop working for many weeks or months. Sick pay is money paid to you by your employer when you are absent because you are unable to work. Statutory Sick Pay (SSP) sets minimum requirements for the level and duration of sick pay; however, many employers provide more generous arrangements. These arrangements are part of your contractual pay and conditions (see pp. 17–19).

Statutory Sick Pay is available to almost all employees. There is no upper age limit or minimum period of service for entitlement. You must, however, earn more than £84 a week (in 2005/06 – this is the lower earnings limit for National Insurance entitlement). Under the scheme, once you have been ill for three working days your employer is required to pay you for each working day you are sick, at a rate equivalent to £70.05 a week.

Entitlement to SSP lasts for up to 28 weeks. After this time your employer is not required to pay you under the statutory scheme but your contractual sick pay period may be longer. If you have a long-term health problem or disability covered by the Disability Discrimination Act your employer may consider whether to extend the period of time you can receive sick pay as part of their duty to consider reasonable adjustments. Even if your employer stops paying you sick pay, they may keep your employment contract open if there is a reasonable prospect of you returning to work.

Claims for sick pay are made by notifying your employer. Your employer will often expect to be notified on the first day of sickness, while to receive SSP you must notify them within a maximum of seven days. During the first week of sickness you do not need evidence from a doctor to receive sick pay although your employer may ask you to fill in a form or certificate yourself. After one week of sickness absence you will be expected to produce medical evidence, in the form of a note or certificate from your GP. If you are unwell for some time, an employer may ask you to see a doctor they have appointed. If they do not believe you are unable to do your job they could refuse to pay you sick pay. If you and your employer disagree about whether you are entitled to SSP for any reason, you have a right to appeal to **HM Revenue and Customs**, who will adjudicate on whether you are entitled to the payment.

If you have two periods of sickness within eight weeks that each lasts more than three days these will be counted as a single sickness period in terms of SSP entitlement. This means that for the second spell of sickness you will not have to wait for three days before being entitled to SSP. However, the downside is that all days of sickness that are linked together count towards the 28 week limit for SSP. If you change jobs the upper limit of 28 weeks still applies.

If you have recently started working after claiming Incapacity Benefit the rules are different. You are expected to claim Incapacity Benefit rather than Statutory Sick Pay for the first 28 weeks of sickness. In addition, if you find work while you were still entitled to the benefit (because you still have a health problem) you will have an automatic right to resume your claim for up to two years after it ends. You will not be entitled to SSP but will instead be paid Incapacity Benefit at the rate you were previously being paid (which may be higher than the level of SSP). However, these rules do not affect your contractual rights to sick pay provided by your employer.

INCOME OPTIONS FOR LONG-TERM SICKNESS

If you are still sick when your entitlement to statutory or contractual sick pay comes to an end, you can make a claim for Incapacity Benefit. You may also be eligible for income under an insurance policy which you can either buy yourself or may be offered by your employer as a benefit. Alternatively, you may be able to start drawing a private or occupational pension, including a pension from your current employer if you agree on ill-health retirement. It is also important that you claim National Insurance credits while you're away from work to ensure you qualify for the state pension.

You can claim National Insurance credits by applying to **Jobcentre Plus**, either as a free-standing application or as part of a claim for benefits. See chapter 12 for information on National Insurance credits.

Often the end of entitlement to sick pay will coincide with the end of your employment contract. However, your employment contract only ends at the point where you agree to resign or you are dismissed. It is possible that your employer will stop paying you sick pay but keep your employment contract open if there is a reasonable prospect of you returning to work. If you are disabled under the terms of the Disability Discrimination Act your employer could consider holding your job open as part of their duty to make reasonable adjustments. Most of your options for income will not be affected by whether you still have an employment contract. The exception is ill-health pensions which are usually only paid if you have retired. However, since it is now possible for you to draw a pension while continuing in employment, your employer may allow you to start drawing a pension with the understanding that you will return to work if your health improves.

Pensions

If your employer offers you ill-health retirement, you will be able to apply for your pension immediately. These days pension schemes are strict in applying the rules on health-related retirement and they may well ask you to take a medical examination and supply your full medical records. Depending on the rules of your scheme, you may be paid the full pension you would have accrued by the time you reached the pension scheme's retirement age. Before you apply for a health-related early retirement pension, you should read your scheme booklet carefully, and ideally consult your trade union to make sure you get the details right. Entitlement to ill-health-related pension does not affect your ability to claim benefits, although it may affect the amount of income you receive.

Social security benefits

When your employer stops paying you sick pay, you will become entitled to claim health-related benefits (even if you still have an employment contract). If you have moved from work you will probably have recent National Insurance contributions which entitle you to claim Incapacity Benefit. For the first six months you will be paid the benefit at the same rate as statutory sick pay. After that your payment will rise to £78.50 a week. Incapacity Benefit is not a means-tested benefit, so your savings will not be affected. However, if you receive a pension of over £85 a week this will lead to a reduction in your benefit (you lose 50p of benefit for every pound of pension over £85 a week). If you have a low income you may be entitled to claim other benefits as well as Incapacity Benefit, for example Income Support, Housing Benefit and Council Tax Benefit.

If you are not moving onto benefits directly from being an employee, your entitlements will probably be different. If you are self-employed you are not eligible for statutory sick pay so, instead, you can claim Incapacity Benefit from the first day of sickness. Similarly, if you are not in work when you become ill you can claim immediately. In these circumstances Incapacity Benefit is paid for six months at a lower rate of £59.20 a week. After that you receive the same amount as if you had entered the benefit from statutory sick pay. If you have not made recent National Insurance contributions you will probably be entitled to Income Support rather than Incapacity Benefit. Income Support is a means-tested benefit so your payments will be reduced to take account of any other income or savings you have. If you are claiming Income Support because of ill-health you will be entitled to an increment. This will take the payment to £81.95 a week.

Initial entitlement to Incapacity Benefit and Income Support is dependent on your doctor certifying that you are not able to work. To remain on the benefit after eight weeks, you are required to attend a medical assessment carried out by doctors working for the Department for Work and Pensions. This is called the Personal Capability Assessment and is based on

World Health Organization criteria for incapacity for work. The way assessments are carried out have often been criticised in the past (eg, where doctors do not take the time to carry out a comprehensive assessment). The government is currently reviewing the assessment, and particularly wants to update the criteria for assessing mental health needs.

There are also separate benefits available if your health problem is specifically caused by working for an employer. Industrial Injuries Disablement Benefit is split into two categories – for accidents and diseases (for example deafness and lung or vibration-related disease). The amount of benefit you will receive will depend on the extent to which you are disabled, according to the government's criteria. The maximum level of benefit is currently £127.10 a week (2006/07).

If you have a severe disability, you may be entitled to other benefits while out of work. Disability Living Allowance is not means-tested or dependent on being out of work. If you are eligible for Income Support you may be able to claim additional premiums for severe disability.

Insurance policies

There are also a range of insurance policies which will pay you money if you have a serious health problem. You may buy the insurance yourself or be offered it by your employer as part of your pay and benefits, and in either case it may be bundled together with life assurance in case of your death. You can make a claim under these policies and receive Incapacity Benefit, since it is not means-tested.

There are several types of insurance. First, there are policies which pay you a monthly income during the time you are unable to work. The technical name for this kind of insurance is permanent health insurance, but policies go by a range of names including income replacement insurance, income protection insurance, long-term disability insurance, disability income insurance or personal disability insurance. With these policies, once you have stopped working you will have to wait for between one month and one year for your entitlement to begin. You will then receive a monthly payment until you return to work or reach an upper age limit (often 65). The income is tax free and can be up to 60 per cent of your previous gross earnings depending on the terms of your policy (although the value of any social security benefits you receive will be subtracted by the insurer). If you are able to start working again part time or on lower pay, the policy will continue to pay you some income to make up part of the difference from your previous earnings. You should check whether the policy will affect your entitlement to means-tested benefits.

Second, there are policies which pay you a lump sum if you have one of a specified list of serious illnesses. These policies are called critical illness insurance. Different policies cover different conditions, but they all include cancer, heart bypass surgery, heart attack, kidney failure, organ transplant, multiple sclerosis and stroke. Certain forms of minor cancer or heart disease will not be covered. Payment is typically made one month after the illness is diagnosed, and can range from £100,000 to £250,000.

Finally, if you are ill because of an accident, you may be eligible for an insurance payment from your employer, your own insurance company or another organisation. If your employer can be shown to be liable they are required to compensate you using compulsory employer's liability insurance. If your accident happened in a public space or building, another organisation may be liable for your injury and may be required to compensate you. In addition, you may be eligible for accident insurance which is not dependent on legal liability for the injury. Many employers have this additional insurance to compensate employees for an accident on their premises irrespective of liability, and your own household or travel insurance may have similar protection. If you receive a compensation payment after a delay in many cases you will be required to pay back any means-tested benefits you would not have been entitled to had you received the money at the time of your accident.

WHAT TO DO AFTER STOPPING WORK

Stopping work because of ill health can be a life-changing event. Most people aged over 50 who stop their job for health reasons expect to get back into work but, unfortunately, the reality is that the majority never work again. If this happens to you, you will almost certainly want to reassess your options and plans for the future. It will often be worth talking to friends and family, including people who have previously been forced to stop working. You should also consider getting professional advice, for example by talking to your GP or contacting a charity that specialises in the health condition you are suffering from.

While your health problem is acute or you are still receiving intensive treatment, your top priority will probably be getting better. But after this initial period, if you have not recovered entirely your health problem will probably stabilise and become a long-term part of your life (this is often described as a 'chronic' health condition). At this point you need to think carefully about your options and what you are going to do. If your health is good enough to avoid it, you probably won't want to spend all day sitting at home watching daytime television. This is because the medical evidence shows that people who lead very inactive lives are likely to become more ill, for example by developing depression or becoming overweight.

On the other hand, many people with long-term health problems worry that if they start to do too much this may make their health worse. There is also an outdated myth that people receiving health-related benefits who start leading an active life, for example by taking part in volunteering or education, will have their benefits taken away. These days the opposite is actually true – **Jobcentre Plus** is very keen to encourage people to be more active.

There are a range of options you could consider. These include taking part in hobbies or leisure activities, becoming a volunteer or getting involved in community organisations, looking after grandchildren, or enrolling for an education course (see chapters 8 and 10). Finally, you may want to consider returning to work, perhaps as an option for the medium term. This could be a return to your previous job or occupation, but you may think that you would be better able to start another job that will be more compatible with maintaining your health, for example becoming self-employed or working part-time.

RETURNING TO WORK

Looking for work

Returning to work after long-term sickness can be daunting, whether you are resuming your previous job or settling into a new one. You may still have health problems and worry that these will be difficult to manage in work, and you're also likely to feel out of touch after a long break.

If you have a long-term health problem or disability, there is now a lot of support to help you get back into work. **Jobcentre Plus** provides a range of services for people receiving health-related benefits, including personal support in looking for work, and access to rehabilitation programmes. Your GP may also be able to refer you to rehabilitation which will help you manage work while having a health problem.

For information on how to look for work see chapter 6. For information on support available from Jobcentre Plus, see chapter 7.

Starting a new job

People who have found a job after a long-term illness often worry about their employer's attitude to ill health. Many people do not tell their new employer about their health history. This is understandable, but it may not be in your best interests. If you tell your employer that you currently have or previously suffered from a long-term health problem they will be put on notice that you are likely to be protected by the Disability Discrimination Act. This means they will be expected to consider what reasonable adjustments should be made to overcome any problems you experience in the work. Making some straightforward adjustments at the outset could be the key to your settling in well. If the adjustment costs money, your employer will be able to apply for government funding under the Access to Work scheme.

If you have returned to work after being out of a job because of ill-health, you may also be eligible for financial support from the government. You are entitled to the disability element of Working Tax Credit if you have been receiving a range of benefits because of your disability (see p. 186 for more details). In some parts of the country you will also be entitled to a £40 a week payment if you find work after a spell on a health-related benefit. This is part of the Pathways to Work scheme, which is now being gradually introduced across the country.

Caring and Family

People aged 50 and over often have to juggle work with family and caring commitments. Many of us enjoy spending time with our families, whether it be grandchildren or children. This can be quite demanding though, as a surprising number of people over the age of 50 are finding that their children are remaining financially – and sometimes emotionally – dependent on them for far longer than used to be the case.

This section does not look at legal rights for parents, because most of these apply only to people with young children. However, you should be aware that if your child is disabled two important rights last until they are 18: the provisions for requesting flexible work and the right to parental leave. Then there are those who are involved in caring for a sick or disabled parent, partner or child. The charity **Carers UK** estimates that there are three million people combining work and this sort of care, so if you're in this situation you're not alone and there *is* support for you.

If you have heavy caring responsibilities you may feel you can't carry on with work, but giving up altogether can be a big step. You will probably have a much lower income and you will lose things you value from work, such as contact with colleagues and job satisfaction. Stopping work could also have implications for your long-term pension situation. You might want to think about other options first. These could include working part time, changing the hours or location of your work, taking longer periods of leave, negotiating a career break where your job is held open, or arranging for support from your local authority, such as a paid care worker.

FLEXIBLE WORKING FOR PEOPLE CARING FOR ADULTS

Flexible working patterns may help you balance work and caring responsibilities. Options could include varying the hours you work, working part time or working from home. If you have a low income as a result of reducing your hours you may be entitled to Carer's Allowance (see below). If you are caring for an adult, many employers will be happy to consider requests to change your working arrangements. Large employers may have a formal policy on flexible working and this could cover carers of adults. But if your employer does not include carers in their policy, or does not have a policy at all, it is still worth asking. Employers have a legal duty to consider flexible working requests from parents and many will accept that it is reasonable to treat carers in the same way. Similarly, if you are providing a lot of care for your grandchildren, your employer may be happy to change your working pattern. If you have actually become the legal guardian of your grandchild you have the same right as a parent.

You may be worried about telling your employer about your caring responsibilities. However, a good employer should be sympathetic. It will be in their interests to help you balance work and caring because anything that helps you keep your job will mean they can avoid spending money on recruiting and training someone to replace you.

From April 2007 the legal process for considering requests for flexible working will be extended to most carers of adults.

The process is sometimes called the 'right to request flexible working' but it is actually a legal requirement for your employer to follow a specified procedure in handling requests to work flexibly. This process only applies if you are classified as an employee (rather than as an agency worker, for example) and have worked for your employer for at least 26 weeks. At the time of writing, the government has not announced who will count as a carer, although it seems likely that carers will be restricted to close relatives or people who live with the person they are caring for.

The statutory process involves you making a written application for flexible working. Your employer must then hold a meeting within 28 days to discuss the request. Following the meeting, your employer must notify you in writing of their decision within 14 days. If your employer refuses your request you can appeal, and your employer must hold another meeting and then give you a final written decision.

APPLICATION CHECKLIST

Assuming the procedure for carers follows the model currently used for parents, in order to follow the statutory process your application must:

- be in writing (whether on paper, email or fax);

- state, that the application is being made under the statutory right to request a flexible working pattern;

- confirm, you are caring for an adult (depending on the detail of the legislation, you may need to state how you are related to the person you are caring for);

- explain what effect, if any, you think the proposed change would have on the employer and how, in your opinion, any such effect might be dealt with;

- specify the flexible working pattern applied for;

- state the date on which it is proposed the change should become effective;

- state whether a previous application has been made to the employer and, if so, when it was made;

- be dated.

Most requests for flexible working are accepted by employers. Your employer is, however, free to turn down your request on one of a number of listed grounds, as long as they explain why the ground is relevant to the circumstances. The reasons for refusing are:

- burden of additional costs;

- detrimental effect on ability to meet customer demand;

- inability to reorganise work among existing staff;

- inability to recruit additional staff;

- detrimental impact on quality;

- detrimental impact on performance;

- insufficiency of work during the periods the employee proposes to work;

- planned structural changes.

If your employer refuses any request you make for flexible working, you may be able to challenge this as discrimination, for example by showing that refusing to offer flexible working to a carer indirectly discriminates against women (sex discrimination) or people aged over 50 (age discrimination) as carers are most likely to be in these groups. The European Court of Justice is currently considering whether carers of disabled people should be protected by the Disability Discrimination Act if they are treated unfavourably for a reason relating to the disability of the person they are caring for. A ruling on this question is not expected until 2008, however. In all these cases an employer can prove they are not discriminating if they are able to justify their decision, although they need to provide good reasons based on evidence.

TIME OFF FOR EMERGENCIES

Employees have a statutory right to take time off to deal with emergencies involving dependants. The statutory right is for unpaid time off but your employer may agree to pay you. The law says you may take off a 'reasonable' period of time; how long this is will depend greatly on the emergency.

DEFINITION OF EMERGENCY

Emergencies must be unexpected or sudden and are defined as situations where someone:

- is ill and needs your help;

- is involved in an accident or assaulted (even if they are not injured);

- needs you to arrange their longer-term care;

- needs you to deal with an unexpected disruption or breakdown in care, such as a care worker or nurse failing to turn up;

- goes into labour (but this does not include you helping after the birth of the child);

- dies (this includes your arranging and attending the funeral).

The law defines a dependant as a parent, child, husband, wife or someone you share your home with (excluding tenants and paid staff). You can also take time off to help another person who is reliant on you, for example where you are their primary carer or the only person on hand to help them in an emergency (although strangely, in these circumstances, the right does not cover death, arranging longer-term care or helping if they go into labour). This means that, in most circumstances, people who care for a sick or disabled adult are covered by the right, even if they do not live with them. If you are a grandparent it is also likely to be reasonable for you to take off time to look after a grandchild, even if you are not their main carer, for example if you work nearby and their parent will take too long to arrive on the scene. If your daughter is giving birth you are automatically covered by the right.

OTHER LEAVE

The right to time off for emergencies is a minimum legal right. However, many employers will be prepared to offer additional leave, either on a paid or unpaid basis. They may offer you compassionate leave if a family member or dependant becomes ill or dies. Sometimes you may be able to negotiate special carer's leave if you know in advance that you will need to be absent at a particular time, for example to help with a hospital appointment (as you knew about this in advance you cannot take time off for an emergency). If you have a disabled child aged under 18 there is also a statutory right to unpaid parental leave once you have a year's service with an employer. You can take four weeks a year, up to a maximum of 18 weeks in total. Finally, if you are unable to take any other leave to carry out caring, you will need to use annual leave.

INCOME

If you have to stop work or reduce your earnings because of caring, you will want to think carefully about how to maximise your income. One option could be to draw an occupational or private pension early (but if you do, this could affect your retirement income). You may also be entitled to financial support from the government. If you are caring for 35 hours or more a week for someone who is receiving Attendance Allowance or Disability

Living Allowance, you may be entitled to Carer's Allowance (it is worth checking whether they are entitled to these benefits if they are not claiming). The allowance will pay you £46.95 a week. It is not means-tested so your entitlement will not be affected if you have a partner who is working; however, there are restrictions based on your earnings or receipt of other benefits

If you are in work you can receive the allowance and earn up to £84 a week. When you calculate your earnings to work out if you are paid less than this threshold, you need only take into account take-home pay (excluding income tax, National Insurance and half your occupational pension contributions). You can also disregard other necessary work-related expenses and half the costs of any care you buy to look after someone while you are at work. With all these exceptions you could be eligible for Carer's Allowance even if your gross earnings are well above £84 a week.

If you are caring and have a low income, you can claim Income Support, while anyone over 60 with a low income is entitled to Pension Credit. If you are also eligible for Carer's Allowance you will not receive the allowance but should receive a premium on your Income Support or Pension Credit instead.

SUPPORT FOR CARING

The person you are caring for is entitled to an assessment of their needs and may be eligible for community care services (each local authority has its own criteria based on level of need, income and savings). If they are eligible for support, the provision they receive must take account of how much care you can offer; so if you are unable or unwilling to provide all the help your friend or relative needs, social services must offer appropriate services instead. For example, if you want to work for part of the week ,social services must provide alternative care if the person you care for is eligible. Often social services departments will be able to offer temporary care so that you can take a holiday.

Local authority social services departments are also required to offer a *carer's assessment* if you are providing care to someone who is sick or disabled and cannot manage without your help. The aim of the assessment is for you to discuss the help you need with caring, and how you can maintain your own health and balance caring with your life, work and family commitments. The assessment must take account of your preferences about work, education, and leisure activities. Social services should not assume that you want to carry on caring in the way that you currently do. This means you can use an assessment as a way of demonstrating what new support you need to be able to carry on working, or to move back into work.

Whether or not the person you are caring for is eligible for support – or has declined help – the social services department can also offer direct support to you as a carer. This might include a taxi fare to help you get to work on time, help with the costs of an adult education course, or counselling to help you cope with the emotional side of caring. Care provided to cover the time you are working is not included, as this counts as a service provided to the person you care for.

If the person you are caring for is not eligible for local authority support, you can buy care from a care services agency yourself. This can be paid for by the person you are caring for (for example using income from their Attendance Allowance) or by yourself (bearing in mind that if you pay for these fees this might take your earnings below the £84 threshold for Carer's Allowance eligibility).

If you want to find out more about services that are available, a local carer support group, such as **Crossroads**, should be able to help. **Carers UK** is a national charity which offers information for carers and can signpost you to a local carers organisation. Your local **Age Concern** will be able to advise you about benefits and services available to an older relative you are caring for.

GIVING UP WORK TO CARE

After looking at all the options, you may conclude that it is just not possible to balance caring with your job. Before you resign, you should see if other options are available, such as taking early retirement or negotiating a career break, with your job held open.

Many people find that being a carer takes up a huge amount of time and it can be very stressful. However, if you can, you should consider finding time each week to do something else, for example a hobby, education course, volunteering, or a few hours of paid work. People who make time for themselves often find it easier to carry on providing care to their friend or relative, and are also better placed to adapt if their circumstances change.

If you decide you want to return to work, **Jobcentre Plus** can provide you with help. If you or your partner receive Income Support, Incapacity Benefit or another benefit, you will probably be eligible for a New Deal programme. There may also be a local scheme designed for carers looking for work run by a charity or carer's organisation. **Carers UK** provides information about help getting back into work as part of their Action for Carers and Employment programme.

Questionnaire of person aggrieved: The Complainant

Note:
- Before filling in this questionnaire, we advise you to prepare what you want to say on a separate piece of paper.
- If you have insufficient room on the questionnaire for what you want to say, continue on an additional piece of paper, which should be sent with the questionnaire to the respondent.

Enter the name of the person to be questioned (the respondent)

To [   ]

Enter the respondent's address

of [   ]

Enter your name (you are the complainant)

1.1 [   ]

Enter your address

of [   ]

Please give as much relevant information as you can about the treatment you think may have been unlawful discrimination. You should mention the circumstances leading up to that treatment and, if possible, give the date, place and approximate time it happened. You should bear in mind that at paragraph 4 of this questionnaire you will be asking the respondent whether he/she agrees with what you say here.

1.2 Consider that you may have discriminated against me and/or subjected me to harassment contrary to the Employment Equality (Age) Regulations 2006.

In paragraph 1.3 you are telling the respondent that you think the treatment you have described in 1.2 may have been unlawful discrimination/ harassmen by them against you. You do not have to complete 1.3. If you do not wish or are unable to do so, you should delete the word 'because'. If you wish to complete paragraph 1.3, but feel you need more information about the Employment Equality (Age) Regulations 2006 before doing so, see the notes attached.

If you do decide to complete paragraph 1.3, you may find it useful to indicate what kind of discrimination/harassment you think the treatment may have been ie. whether it was:
- direct discrimination;
- indirect discrimination;
- harassment; or
- victimisation;

1.3 I consider that this treatment may have been unlawful because:

and which provision of the regulations you think may make unlawful the kind of discrimination you think you may have suffered.

This is the first of your questions to the respondent. You are advised not to alter it.

This is the second of your questions to the respondent. You are advised not to alter it.

• The questions at paragraph 3 are especially important if you think you may have suffered direct discrimination, or indirect discrimination because they ask the respondent whether your age had anything to do with your treatment. They do not ask specific questions relating to victimisation. Questions at paragraph 4 provide you with the opportunity to ask other questions you think may be of importance. For example, if you think you have been discriminated against by having been refused a job, you may want to know what the qualifications were of the person who did get the job and why that person got the job.

If you think you have been victimised you may find it helpful to include the following questions:

• Was the reason for my treatment the fact that I had done or intended to do, or that you suspected I had done or intended to do, any of the following:

• brought proceedings under the Employment Equality (Age) Regulations 2006;

• gave evidence or information in connection with proceedings under the regulations;

• did something else under or by reference to the regulations; or

• made an allegation that someone acted unlawfully under the regulations

2. Do you agree that the statement in 1.2 above is an accurate description of what happened? If not, in what respect do you disagree or what is your version of what happened?

3. Do you accept that your treatment of me was unlawful discrimination/ harassment by you against me? If not:
   a) why not,
   b) for what reason did I receive the treatment accorded to me, and
   c) how far did considerations of age affect your treatment of me?

4. Any other questions you may wish to ask:

5. My address for any reply you may wish to give to the questions I have raised is:

At 1 above ☐ below ☐
(please tick appropriate box)

The questionnaire must be signed and dated. If it is to be signed on behalf of (rather than by) the complainant, the person signing should:

- describe himself/herself e.g. 'solicitor acting for (name of complainant)'; and

- give business address (or home address, if appropriate).

Signed

Date

Address (if appropriate)

How to serve the papers

- We strongly advise that you retain and keep in a safe place a copy of the completed questionnaire.

- Send the person to be questioned the whole of this document either to their usual last known residence or place of business or if you know they are acting through a solicitor, to that address. If your questions are directed at a limited company or other corporate body or a trade union or employers' association, you should send the papers to the secretary or clerk at the registered or principal office. You should be able to find out where this is by enquiring at your public library. However, if you are unable to do so you will have to send the papers to the place where you think it is most likely they will reach the secretary or clerk. It is your responsibility to see that they receive them.

- You can deliver the papers in person or send them by post.

- If you send them by post, we advise you to use the recorded delivery service (this will provide you with proof of delivery).

By virtue of regulation 41 of the Employment Equality (Age) Regulations 2006 this questionnaire and any reply are (subject to the provisions of that regulation) admissible in proceedings under the Regulations. A court or tribunal may draw any such inference as is just and equitable from a failure without reasonable excuse to reply within eight weeks of service of this questionnaire, or from an evasive or equivocal reply, including an inference that the person questioned has committed an unlawful act.

REPLY: THE RESPONDENT

Note:
- Before completing this reply form, we advise you to prepare what you want to say on a separate piece of paper.
- If you have insufficient room on the reply form for what you want to say, continue on an additional piece of paper, which should be attached to the reply form and sent to the complainant.

Enter the name of the person you are replying to (the complainant)

To [   ]

Enter the complainant's address

of [   ]

Enter your name (you are the respondent).

1. [   ]

Enter your address

of [   ]

Complete as appropriate

hereby acknowledge receipt of the questionnaire signed by you and dated

[   ]

which was served on me on (date)

[   ]

Please tick relevant box: If you **disagree** with the complainant's statement of events, you should explain in what respects you disagree, or your version of what happened, or both.

2. I agree ☐ that the statement in 1.2 of the questionnaire is an accurate description of what happened.

I disagree ☐ with the statement in 1.2 of the questionnaire in that:

[   ]

Please tick relevant box: you are answering question at paragraph 3 of the complainant's questionnaire here. If, in answer to paragraph 2 of the questionnaire you have agreed that the statement is an accurate description of what happened but dispute that it is an unlawful discrimination, you should state your reasons. If you have **disagreed** with the facts in the complainant's statement of events, you should answer the question on the basis of your version of the facts. We advise you to look at the attached notes and also the relevant parts of the Employment Equality (Age) Regulations 2006. You will need to know:

- how the regulations define discrimination and in what situations the regulations make discrimination unlawful – see paragraph 1 of the attached notes; and

- what exceptions the regulations provide – see paragraph 3 of the attached notes.

If you think that an exception (eg. the exception for employment where a person's age is a genuine occupational qualification) applies to the treatment described in paragraph 1. 2 of the complainant's questionnaire, you should mention this in paragraph 3a, with an explanation about why you think the exception applies.

Delete the whole of this sentence if you have answered all the questions in the complainant's questionnaire. If you are unable or unwilling to answer the questions please tick the appropriate box and give your reasons for not answering them.

The reply form must be signed and dated. If it is to be signed on behalf of (rather than by) the respondent the person signing should:
- describe himself/herself eg.'solicitor acting for (name of respondent)' or 'personnel manager of (name of firm)'; and
- give business address (or home address if appropriate).

3a. I accept ☐ that my treatment of you was unlawful discrimination [harassment] by me against you.

I dispute ☐ that my treatment of you was unlawful discrimination [harassment] by me against you. My reasons for so disputing are:

3b. The reason why you received the treatment accorded to you and the answers to the other questions in paragraph 3 of the questionnaire are:

4. Replies to questions in paragraph 4 of the questionnaire:

5. I have deleted (in whole or in part) the paragraphs numbered above
since I am unable ☐
since I am unwilling ☐
to reply to the relevant questions in the complainant's questionnaire for the reasons given in the box below.

Signed
Date
Address (if appropriate)

Glossary

Access to Learning Fund Money students in higher education can apply for if they face hardship.

Additional voluntary contributions Voluntary contributions to an occupational pension in addition to your normal payments.

Age (discrimination) regulations The Employment Equality (Age) Regulations 2006, outlawing age discrimination from October 2006.

Annuity A financial product that converts a pension fund or other savings into a regular guaranteed income, usually for the rest of your life.

Civil partnership A legal partnership between two people of the same sex. Has similar status to marriage between two people of opposite sexes.

Claimant A person bringing a claim at the employment tribunal.

Compromise agreement A contractual agreement between an employer and a worker to settle an employment dispute, under which the worker agrees not to bring any legal action against the employer, usually in return for financial compensation.

Constructive dismissal The resignation of an employee as a result of a fundamental breach of the employment contract on the part of the employer. The resignation is seen as a dismissal for the purposes of claiming unfair dismissal.

Contracting 'in' and 'out' If you have a personal or occupational pension you either pay National Insurance contributions at the full rate ('contracting in') or pay a reduced rate ('contracting out'), as part of the terms of the pension.

Criminal Records Bureau (CRB) A check employers are required to carry out when recruiting for people to work with children or vulnerable people, to find out if applicants have a criminal record.

Curriculum vitae (CV) A document summarising a person's qualifications, skills and experience used when applying for a job.

Default retirement age Set by the government at 65, this is the age above which an employer may force an employee to retire, as long as the retirement is procedurally correct.

Defined benefit pension *see* salary-related pension.

Defined contribution pension A type of occupational or personal pension where the pension contributions are paid into an investment fund. When you retire the fund is used to buy an annuity which gives you an income for the rest of your life.

Direct discrimination Treating one person less favourably than another on the grounds of their age, race, sex, disability, sexual orientation, or religion or belief.

Disability premium A supplement added to social security benefits if you are disabled (eg Income Support, Council Tax Benefit, Housing Benefit).

Earnings Threshold The minimum amount of weekly pay you need to earn before you pay National Insurance contributions. This is higher than the Lower Earnings Limit; if your earnings are between the LEL and the Earnings Threshold you build up National Insurance entitlement without having to pay contributions yourself.

Employee Someone who works under a contract of employment.

Employment tribunal The judicial body, similar to a court, which decides claims based on disputes between employers and employees.

Equity release mortgage A financial product that involves a mortgage company taking a stake in your home, in exchange for paying you money.

Final salary pension A type of salary-related pension where your pension is calculated on the basis of the salary you earn in the last year in your job.

Flexible working Any working pattern that is non-standard in your workplace. This could include part-time work, adjusted working hours and home working. From April 2007 carers of adults have a right to request flexible working.

Genuine Occupational Requirement An exception to the general principle of non-discrimination when a certain characteristic – such as gender or race – is really necessary for a person to be able to do a particular job.

Guarantee Credit Part of Pension Credit available to anyone aged over 60 which guarantees you a minimum weekly income.

Harassment Behaviour which violates another person's dignity, or creates *an intimidating, hostile, degrading, humiliating or offensive environment* for them, whether on purpose or by accident, and which is based on their age, sex, race, disability, sexual orientation, religion or belief.

Home Responsibilities Protection A system for building up entitlement to the basic state pension for parents looking after children and carers of disabled adults.

Incapacity Benefit The main social security benefit for people who are unable to work because of ill health or disability.

Income Support Benefit for people who are out of work, have a low income, and are not actively seeking work; for example, people who are sick or disabled, or carers.

Income Tax personal allowance The amount of income you are entitled to tax-free, before income tax is levied. Most people aged over 65 have a higher personal allowance than younger adults.

Independent financial adviser Services offering regulated expert advice on financial products which are not linked to any particular company.

Indirect discrimination The application of a provision, criterion or practice which puts persons of a particular age group, sex, race, sexual orientation, religion or belief at a particular disadvantage when compared with other persons.

Jobseeker's Agreement A document that recipients of Jobseeker's Allowance must agree which sets out the steps they will take to find work.

Jobseeker's Allowance Benefit for people below state pension age who are unemployed and who are actively seeking work.

Learner Support Fund Money students at further education colleges can apply for if they have a low income or face hardship.

Lower Earnings Limit (LEL) The minimum amount of weekly pay you need to earn to build up National Insurance contributions.

National Minimum Wage The minimum amount anyone can be paid for each hour they work. In October 2006 the minimum wage for adults was £5.35.

Normal retirement age The age at which it is customary for employees in a particular position to retire: usually the same as the contractual retirement age but not always. If in practice people are normally required to retire at a different age, that will be the normal retirement age. It may be that there is no normal retirement age for a position.

Occupational pension A pension operated by your employer. They can be defined as contribution or salary-related pensions. Not all pensions offered by employers are occupational pensions as employers can also arrange a personal pension that you buy from an insurance company.

Pension Credit a social security benefit for people aged over 60 with low or moderate incomes.

Permitted work Work that can be carried out by a person in receipt of an incapacity-related benefit without it affecting their entitlement to the benefit.

Personal pension A pension bought from an insurance company (although it may be arranged by your employer). Examples include Stakeholder Pensions and Group Personal Pensions. They are always defined contribution pensions.

Positive action Action to compensate for disadvantages faced by people of a particular age, sex, race, sexual orientation, religion or belief, which improves access to training and encourages people to take up employment opportunities.

Redundancy The dismissal of an employee because the work they do is no longer needed, or their position no longer exists.

Respondent A person, or organisation, against whom a claim is brought at the employment tribunal.

Retirement age The age at which an employee retires.

Salary-related pension A type of occupational pension where your employer pays you a pension calculated according with reference to your earnings and length of service.

Savings Credit Part of Pension Credit available to anyone aged over 65 which tops up any income you have from earnings, savings or private pensions.

Self-assessment tax return A tax return for self-employed people or people with complicated financial affairs to declare their income.

Self-employed Someone who works under a contract for services and is neither an employee nor a worker. The arrangements for National Insurance and Income Tax are different for self-employed people compared to workers.

Stakeholder pensions A simple type of personal pension which most employers must offer if they do not have another type of pension. The government sets limits on the maximum fees insurance companies may charge.

State pension age The age from which a person is entitled to receive state pension: currently 60 for women and 65 for men. It will rise gradually to 65 for women between 2010 and 2010.

State Pension Forecast A Pension Service prediction of how much state pension you are likely to receive when you reach state pension age, based on your past and current National Insurance contributions.

Unfair dismissal A dismissal which is unlawful because it was made without a fair reason, or was procedurally unfair.

Upper earnings level The maximum amount of weekly pay on which you need to pay National Insurance at the standard rate. You must pay 1% National Insurance on any additional earnings.

Victimisation Less favourable treatment of a person because they have made a complaint of discrimination or given evidence in support of someone else's complaint.

Worker Someone who works under a contract to personally perform work but who is not a self-employed person providing services for a customer. Includes employees, contract workers, casual workers and agency workers.

Working Tax Credit A tax credit providing additional income for people who are in work but who have a low income, disability or children.

Wrongful dismissal A dismissal in breach of the contract of employment.

List of Useful Organisations

Advice UK
For help locating an independent
advice agency in your area.
Telephone: 020 7407 4070
www.adviceuk.org.uk

**Advisory, Conciliation and
Arbitration Service (ACAS)**
Provides advice and information
on your rights at work as well as
conciliation service in employment
disputes.
Telephone: 08457 47 47 47
www.acas.org.uk

**The Age and Employment
Network (TAEN)**
A network of partners working to
remove age barriers to opportunity,
for individuals wanting to work or
learn, and for organisations.
Telephone: 020 7843 1590
www.taen.org.uk

Age Positive
A campaign run by the Department
for Work & Pensions promoting age
diversity in employment.
Email: agepositive.@dwp.gsi.gov.
uk
www.agepositive.gov.uk

**Association of British
Correspondence Colleges**
For details of distance learning
courses and colleges.
Telephone: 020 8544 9559
www.homestudy.org.uk

Benefit Enquiry Line
Provides advice and information
about benefits and how to claim
them for disabled people and carers.
Telephone: 0800 88 22 00

Business Link
For advice and training on starting
up a business.
Telephone: 0845 600 9006
www.businesslink.gov.uk
Look in your local phone book for
your nearest Business Link.

Carers UK
A campaigning organisation that
provides information and advice
for carers. Carers UK also leads the
ACE National (Action for Carers
and Employment) partnership.
Carers line: 0808 808 7777
www.carersuk.org
www.acecarers.org.uk

Citizens Advice (CAB)
Free independent information and advice, including employment advice.
www.citizensadvice.org.uk
See your local phone book for details of your nearest Citizens Advice Bureau.

Commission for Equality and Human Rights (CEHR)
Responsible for tackling discrimination, including on grounds of age, and promoting human rights. Expected to be operational from October 2007.
www.cehr.org.uk

Community Legal Service Direct
A helpline for people who qualify for legal aid. The website includes a directory of legal information and advice providers.
Telephone: 0845 345 4345
www.clsdirect.org.uk

Companies House
An organisation that administers limited companies in Britain.
Telephone: 0870 33 33 636
Minicom@ 02920 381245
www.companieshouse.gov.uk

CREATE
Impartial advice for people considering self-employment through franchising.
Telephone: 01727 813 747
www.createproject.org.uk

Crossroads
An organisation that runs local schemes to provide practical support for carers. Use the website to find your local scheme.
Telephone: 0845 450 0350
www.crossroads.org.uk

Department of Trade and Industry (DTI)
The government department responsible for trade, business, employees, consumers, science and energy.
Telephone: 020 7215 5000
Minicom: 020 7215 6740
Email: dtienquiries@dti.gsi.gov.uk
www.dti.gov.uk

Department for Work and Pensions (DWP)
The government department dealing with employment, benefits and pensions, it is responsible for the **Jobcentre Plus** website and offices and for the **Pension Service**.
Telephone: 020 7712 2171
www.dwp.gov.uk

Directgov
A website that brings together a wide range of public service information from government departments.
www.direct.gov.uk

Disability Rights Commission

Provides information and advice on rights under the Disability Discrimination Act.
DRC, Freepost MID02164, Stratford upon Avon, CV37 9BR
Telephone: 08457 622 633
www.drc.org.uk

Do-it.org.uk

National database of volunteering opportunities.
Telephone: 020 7226 8008
www.do-it.org.uk

Educational Grants Advisory Service

For guidance and advice on funding for adult learning, including a database of trusts and charities that assist students.
Telephone: 020 7254 6251
www.egas-online.org

Employers Forum on Age

A network of employers promoting age diversity in the workforce. It provides information on the age discrimination law for employers.
Telephone: 0845 456 2495
www.efa.org.uk

Employment Agency Standards Inspectorate (part of the Department of Trade and Industry)

For complaints against employment agencies.
Telephone: 0845 955 5105
Minicom: 020 7215 6740

Employment Tribunals Service

If you want to make a claim against an employer at a tribunal.
Telephone: 0845 795 9775
Minicom: 0845 757 3722
www.employmenttribunals.gov.uk

Financial Services Authority (FSA)

The independent regulator of the financial services industry, it provides information for consumers on a wide range of financial matters, including pensions.
Telephone: 0845 606 1234
www.fsa.gov.uk

Health and Safety Executive

For information and guidance about health and safety at work
Telephone: 0845 345 0055
www.hse.gov.uk

HM Revenue & Customs

If you need to submit a self-assessment tax return or claim tax credits you can do so online at their website. There's also a helpline for the newly self-employed (see below).
Telephone: 08459 154 515
www.hmrc.gov.uk

Help the Aged

A charity that provides a wide range of information for older people.
Telephone: 0808 800 6565
www.helptheaged.org.uk

IFA Promotion Ltd
An organisation that provides details of local independent financial advisers.
Telephone: 0800 085 3250
www.unbiased.co.uk

Insolvency Service's Redundancy Payments Office
To claim a redundancy payment if your employer has become insolvent.
Telephone: 0845 145 0004
www.insolvency.gov.uk

Jobcentre Plus
Powered by the DWP, it can help with benefit claims and job-hunting and administers a number of government initiatives including Pathways to Work and Work Based Learning for Adults.
Jobseekers Direct provides details of job vacancies.
Telephone: 0845 6060 234
See your local phone book for details of your nearest Jobcentre Plus.
www.jobcentreplus.gov.uk

Law Centres Federation
Can provide a free and independent professional legal service. Check your local phone book to see if there is a law centre in your area.
Telephone: 020 7387 8570
www.lawcentres.org.uk

Law Society of England and Wales
Can help you find a solicitor in your area.
Telephone: 0870 606 6575
www.lawsociety.org.uk

Learndirect
Online courses, local learning centres and careers advice and guidance.
Telephone: 0800 100 900
www.learndirect.co.uk

Life Academy
A charity helping people plan for the future. They offer pre-retirement courses.
Telephone: 01483 301170
www.life-academy.co.uk

National Association for Voluntary and Community Action (NAVCA)
An organisation promoting local voluntary and community action.
Telephone: 0114 278 6636
www.navca.org.uk

National Institute for Continuing and Adult Education (NIACE)
An organisation that promotes adult learning. Can provide information on age discrimination in education.
Telephone: 0116 204 4200
www.niace.org.uk

National Minimum Wage Helpline
For help and advice on the minimum wage.
Telephone: 08456 000 678

nextstep
A network of local services providing information and advice about learning and work.
www.nextstep.org.uk
See your local phone book to find your nearest nextstep.

Ofsted
For inspection reports on further education colleges.
Telephone: 08456 40 40 45
www.ofsted.gov.uk

The Open and Distance Learning Quality Council (ODLQC)
Provides advice on learning and courses from a distance.
Telephone: 020 7612 7090
www.odlqc.org.uk

Open University (OU)
A well-known organisation providing university-level distance learning courses.
Telephone: 0870 333 4340
www.open.ac.uk

The Pension Service (part of the DWP)
A government service that provides information for individuals about pensions and some benefits.
Telephone: 0845 606 0265
State Pension Forecasting Team: 0845 3000 168

Pension Tracing Service:
0845 6002 537
To apply for Pension Credit:
0800 99 1234
To claim state pension:
0845 300 1084
www.thepensionservice.gov.uk

The Pensions Advisory Service
An independent voluntary organisation providing information and guidance on state, company, stakeholder and personal pension schemes.
Telephone: 0845 601 2923
www.opas.org.uk

Pension Protection Fund
A fund to compensate members of pension schemes on the insolvency of employers.
Telephone: 0845 600 2541
www.pensionprotectionfund.gov.uk

PRIME
A national organisation dedicated to helping people aged over 50 set up in business.
Telephone: 0800 783 1904
www.primeinitiative.org.uk

REACH
Brings together voluntary organisations and experienced people who want to offer their career skills as volunteers.
Telephone: 020 7582 6543
www.reach-online.org.uk

Retired and Senior Volunteer Programme (RSVP)
Information on volunteering activities for people over 50.
www.csv.org.uk/Volunteer/
Senior+Volunteer

Social Enterprise Coalition
A national organisation supporting and promoting social enterprise.
www.socialenterprise.org.uk

TimeBank UK
Provides information for volunteers and a directory of volunteering opportunities.
Telephone: 0845 456 1668
www.timebank.org.uk

Trades Union Congress (TUC)
Made up of 66 affiliated unions representing nearly seven million working people from all walks of life, they campaign for fair deals for workers.
Telephone: 020 7636 4030
www.tuc.org.uk
See also **Worksmart**.

Train to Gain
A service to help employers get the right training for their staff.
Telephone: 0870 900 6800
www.traintogain.gov.uk

The Universities and Colleges Admissions Service (UCAS)
For information about higher education, universities and colleges, and the admissions process.
Telephone: 0870 11 222 11
www.ucas.com

Workplace Health Connect
A service for small and medium sized businesses, run in partnership with the Health and Safety Executive, providing free practical advice on workplace health and safety.
Telephone: 0845 609 6006
www.workplacehealthconnect.co.uk

www.Worksmart.org.uk
A TUC website giving information on employment rights. The site includes the Union Finder search function allowing you to find if a union is recognised by your employer, or to find a union relevant to the sector you work in.
Union finder telephone: 0870 600 4 882

Volunteering Initiative for the Third Age (VITA)
An organisation that promotes volunteering for people over 65.
Telephone: 01235 442961
www.vitavolunteering.org.uk or
www.v-word.org.uk

Volunteer Centre Network Scotland
See your local phone book for details of your local volunteer centre.
www.volunteerscotland.info

Volunteer Development Agency – Northern Ireland
Telephone: 028 9023 6100
www.volunteering-ni.org

Volunteering England

Look in your local phone book for details of your nearest Volunteer Bureau or Volunteer Centre.
Telephone: 0845 305 6979
www.volunteering.org.uk

Voluntary Service Overseas (VSO)

For information about opportunities to volunteer overseas.
Telephone: 020 8780 7500
www.vso.org.uk

Wales Council for Voluntary Action

www.wcva.org.uk or www.volunteering-wales.net
Look in your local phone book to find your nearest volunteer bureau.

Index

About Age Concern

Age Concern is the UK's largest organisation working for and with older people to enable them to make more of life. A federation of over 400 independent charities that share the same name, values and standards, we believe that later life should be fulfilling, enjoyable and productive.

We undertake research, influence government and media, and work on a variety of innovative and dynamic projects. On a daily basis we provide vital services for thousands of older people of all ages and backgrounds, as well as essential information and support on a wide range of issues.

Age Concern England
1268 London Road
London, SW16 4ER
Tel: 020 8765 7200
www.ageconcern.org.uk

Age Concern Scotland
Causewayside House
160 Causewayside
Edinburgh, EH9 1PP
Tel: 0845 833 0200
www.ageconcernscotland.
org.uk

Age Concern Cymru
Ty John Pathy
Units 13 and 14 Neptune Court
Vanguard Way
Cardiff, CF24 5PJ
Tel: 029 2043 1555
www.accymru.org.uk

Age Concern Northern Ireland
3 Lower Crescent
Belfast, BT7 1NR
Tel: 028 9024 5729
www.ageconcernni.org

Age Concern Factsheets: we produce a range of comprehensive factsheets designed to answer many of the questions that older people – or those advising them – may have. These free factsheets cover issues such as housing, care homes, pensions, benefits, health, community care, leisure and education, and can be obtained by calling our free information line on 0800 00 99 66 or by downloading them from the website: www.ageconcern.org.uk.

Age Concern Books

Age Concern publishes a range of valuable handbooks that provide practical, expert advice on a number of issues. Among other things, our books help thousands of people claim the benefits they are entitled to; make sense of their pensions; cut down on tax payments; plan for their retirement; and look after their health. We also publish user-friendly books on computing and using the internet, as well as how to care for someone suffering from a specific health problem, for example depression, hearing loss, cancer or a stroke.

To find out more, to order a free catalogue or to buy a book please call our hotline on 0870 44 22 120 or visit the website on www.ageconcern.org.uk/bookshop. You can also obtain our books through all good bookshops.

OTHER BOOKS IN THE *YOUR RIGHTS* SERIES...

Your Rights 2006/07:
A guide to money benefits for older people
By Sally West

Your Rights has long established itself as *the* money benefits guide for older people. Updated annually and written in clear, jargon-free language, it will guide you through the complexities of the state benefits and financial support that may be available. If you want to know what you're entitled to and how to claim it, this book is for you.

£5.99 + postage and packing   **0 86242 415 1**

Your Rights to Health Care:
Helping older people get the best from the NHS
By Lorna Easterbrook

Many people are unsure what NHS services they're entitled to. Help is at hand with this comprehensive guide written specifically for the over 60s. It covers all the questions that are likely to arise in a range of situations, from visiting your GP to arranging long-term care for an illness. Whether you – or someone you know – are coping with hearing loss, a mental health issue or a disability, this book will help you get the best from the services available.

£7.99 + postage and packing   **0 86242 398 8**

Understanding taxes and savings 2006/07:
Make more of your money
By Paul Lewis

Many millions of pounds are lost each year through bad savings and overpayment of taxes. Some of us don't realise this is happening, while others don't know how to put it right. Paul Lewis, the acclaimed journalist and broadcaster, is here to help. In his down-to-earth handbook he shows how to avoid paying too much tax while saving enough money for a comfortable and enjoyable retirement.

£7.99 + postage and packing   **0 86242 417 8**

Your guide to pensions 2006/07:
Planning ahead to boost retirement income
By Sue Ward

For many people of working age, planning for retirement is an increasingly important issue. If you're one of the growing numbers of people who are keen to improve their income in later life, you couldn't do better than turn to Sue Ward's practical handbook for help. Updated annually, it explains all major types of pension schemes as well as other forms of retirement income.

£7.99 + postage and packing   **0 86242 418 6**

Choices in retirement:
Your guide to the essentials
By Ro Lyon

Retirement these days means new choices and opportunities. Once you – or your partner – have finally left work, a whole new life awaits you. Whatever dreams, plans and worries you may have, Ro Lyon's friendly and sensible book is here to help. Designed to be of use to those approaching retirement as well as to people who've already left work, it's the book you won't want to do without: a complete guide to a golden opportunity enjoyed to the full.

£9.99 + postage and packing   **0 86242 412 7**